FACE THE

MW00978567

"Nancy's memoir is one of the most spirit moving reads. She possesses a very strong will to complete everything she sets a goal to. Motivational and fun describes this woman and after you begin to read her story, you will not want to put it down."

Dawn Jess, Annie's Books and Gifts
Venice, Florida

"An inspirational journey of self-discovery and triumph over emotional and physical battles."

Ed Jordan, Photographer, Venetian Arts
Sarasota, Florida

"I enjoyed my second reading of your book as much as my first. Your writing style is unpretentious but very descriptive and it drew me into your story. I didn't want it to end."

Judy Gamel, City Management Executive Assistant
Venice, Florida

"I met Nancy in 1999. Her faith and passion for riding a motorcycle has made her solo journey an amazing adventure. I love her fearless and free style of writing!"

Bob Poneleit, Owner, Hap's Cycle Sales
Sarasota, Florida

FACE THE FEAR TOUR

FACE THE FEAR TOUR

Copyright © 2016 by Nancy Taylor

Printed in the United States of America

ISBN: 978-0-578-18644-3

FACE THE FEAR TOUR

Finding Your Inner Strength Through Troubled Times

Nancy Taylor

DEDICATION

This book is dedicated to my mother, Carleen, who always supported my dreams and never underestimated my capabilities!

INTRODUCTION

This motorcycle tour came to fruition out of the fear that totally engulfed me once diagnosed with the Silent Killer: Osteoporosis. My condition was at an advanced stage and I was told that my bones were so brittle that I could fracture at any time just walking. After three months of anguish and panic, I awoke in the middle of the night when a voice came to me and exclaimed: "face your fear!" This voice seemed to have come straight from the heavens, so I knew at that point that I had to make a plan to strengthen my resolve and bring awareness of this disease to others.

I want to share a little bit of my history with the disease that has threatened my independence and livelihood. I was diagnosed, prematurely, at 40 years old, with Osteopenia, and though this was unusual at such a young age, I was not too alarmed. I thought that I would just follow the doctor's orders and with supplements, weight training, and physical activity, I would be able to arrest it. At that time, 1200 mg of Calcium plus Vitamin D was the "magic pill". I felt with this, and my exercise regimen, that I would be covered. At 51 years old, I had a fall from a 12-foot loft and fractured several bones. It was then that I was diagnosed at an early stage of Osteoporosis and my doctor prescribed a monthly medication to help prevent any further bone loss. Every two years I had a bone density test, and even though I had done everything possible to improve my condition, I continued to decline. Now I am at a "high risk for fracture" of my lumbar spine and hip bones. When I received that diagnosis in January of 2015, I was shocked and confused since I was in the best physical shape of my adult life. After three doctor's opinions, I was told that the only treatment left was to have a preventative infusion as a final attempt to increase my life span. This was a drug given to bone cancer patients, and though there was no guarantee that it would make any difference for me, some Osteoporosis patients that were "over the threshold" had seen some results. The problem with this treatment is that it is a very misleading short-term solution. It can only be taken for 5 years and carries with it several disturbing side effects. I also found out through further research that it does not grow new flexible bone. It only hardens the old existing bone. So it worsens the condition of the bones, causing them to become even more brittle overtime. The doctor at the chemotherapy lab, who then ordered the injection, said to me: "Ms. Taylor, you have the bones of an 85 year old woman and with the rate that your bones are disintegrating, you will likely be in a wheel chair from a large bone fracture within three years. It bugs me that this is happening to you at such a young age and it doesn't make any sense!" As I sat in the treatment room, while waiting for the nurse to administer the shot, I was totally consumed with fear as I tried to process the reality of my condition. She then, very solemnly, looked down at me and asked if I had heard all of the horror stories about the drug, and if I wanted to continue with the injection. I was terribly frightened, but had been told that it was my last resort. I left there feeling as if I had just eaten the poison apple!

When I was only 29 years old, I had to have a total hysterectomy. I was then put on synthetic estrogen as a supplement to help maintain bone density. Though, since my aunt had recently died at a very young age from breast cancer, I was given the lowest dose possible to prevent me from possibly acquiring it. Obviously, this was not enough to protect my bones long term. Statistics have proven that more women die from complications of Osteoporosis than breast cancer, so logically it was a toss-up. My theory is that in the real world, "boobs" are held in much higher regard than "bones"!

One of the side effects of the infusion that I took only out of sheer desperation, is that it can weaken the immune system. Shortly, thereafter, I caught a cold, which turned into bronchial pneumonia. I thought for sure that my tour would have to be cancelled. But after three months of intensive treatment, and though physically weak, I put away my breathing machine and began to get ready to hit the road.

Since my diagnosis, I had experienced many emotions, but the most crippling of them all was the fear of being disabled or premature loss of life. Every step that I took could be the one when a large bone fractured and my active life as I knew it would be over, forever. I was shocked when my research uncovered the fact that Osteoporosis came with a much higher, overall, mortality rate than breast, ovarian and uterine cancer combined. The risk of dying from a large bone fracture is also greater than that of death from gastric or pancreatic cancer. Pneumonia takes the lives of 25% of the victims within just one year of being incapacitated!

It was after my fall from the loft that I discovered ballet as a means to repair my body. At 52 years old I limped into a ballet studio and with the help from the instructor, I began something that would change my mind, body, and soul forever. At 57 years old I began teaching myself pointe (to dance on toes). Learning to dance "en pointe" at such an advanced age is mostly unheard of, but a challenge that I was enjoying tremendously. I just could not give up and allow the joy of dance be taken away from me, since from then on I knew that I would be dancing for my life!

The main purpose of my trip would be to promote the

awareness of Osteoporosis (which not only affects the young and the old, but men and women alike) and to encourage others to get a bone density test early in life.

Though I realized that I had lacked the knowledge that may have protected me from such a debilitating and life threatening disease, I had hoped that I might turn it into a positive experience by eliminating the suffering of others.

Motorcycling for over 40 years had always been a source of strength and empowerment for me. So what better way to regain my courage and become fearless than to do a cross country tour on my bike, alone, facing the unknown and the tremendous challenges that such an experience might bring?

My very first ride on the back of a motorcycle was when I was nine years old. We were up at the lake and a friend of the family was a State Trooper in the motorcycle division, who was then off duty and giving rides to the children vacationing there. When my turn came, I knew that it was the most exhilarating thing that had ever happened to me in my life thus far. I was bitten by the adventure bug on that day, and was driven to pursue my dream of someday riding on my own.

I have had the privilege of enjoying six different motorcycles in my lifetime. At age fifteen I shared the fun of riding a mini bike that belonged to my younger brother. When I was seventeen I had saved enough money to buy a "real motorcycle" that I thought I could take on the open road. It was only 100cc and without my mother's knowledge, I took to the interstate even though I knew that it was extremely dangerous with a bike that small! At eighteen, I traded in my "little bike" for a 350cc and ventured further out to places beyond my hometown. But when I bought my 400cc bike, I took off for California! A few years passed without a bike when I had sold my last one to buy a sailboat. For ten years I lived on my boat, traveling up and down the East and West coasts of Florida. Once a landlubber, again, I purchased a 250cc motorcycle to hold me over while I searched for the last motorcycle that I would ever own. It took a while to find the perfect bike, but the day that I slid into the saddle of my 600cc Shadow, I knew immediately that it was the one! Every time that I start up my bike, hear the roar of its engine, and feel its power beneath me, it still sends a chill up my spine!

PREPARATIONS

I had my motorcycle serviced and checked for safety with my departure date scheduled for June 11th. God willing. Hopefully, I would be ready to get on the road with plans to travel 4,000 miles within 30 days. My route would take me from my home in Florida, on through Georgia, Tennessee, Kentucky, and Indiana, with my destination being Michigan's Upper Peninsula, and returning by way of Ohio, West Virginia, Virginia, North Carolina, South Carolina and once again, through Georgia and back into Florida. I would be tent camping when the weather permitted, allowing me to touch more souls along the way.

I did part of my pre-trip strengthening exercises at my community pool, and it was there that I partook in a discussion with a retired nurse about my cause to bring awareness to Osteoporosis. She did not share in my enthusiasm on the subject for she said: "they are just bones!" She then went on to elaborate about all of her 40 years in nursing. I could only wonder how her education would have excluded the knowledge and the need for healthy bones in order to survive!

A large part of the preparation for my trip included researching for and finding all of the safety gear possible that I would need in hopes of returning home in one piece! I have always taken this part of motorcycling quite seriously and realized that my old gear needed major updating. I was amazed at the modern technology that was available on the Internet, though I ran into a very big problem immediately upon trying to place my first order. I am a petite, size 2 and all of the women's gear began at a size 4 or a size 6 for clothing and all of the boots only came in a medium width. This began a series of ordering each item of gear from multiple companies in search of a size 4 that ran smaller than the rest, and boots with the narrowest width. For three months, I either had packages being delivered to my door, or I was shipping them back. I found myself on a first name basis with all of the delivery men!

I packed up my motorcycle with 100# of gear and did my test run. Though it was obvious that the extra weight would be a very difficult challenge for me, the bike handled great! Hopefully, I had thought of everything that I would need for a one month tour. I know that I laid  awake many long nights thinking about the details! And even though I had carefully planned out my trip, it would be "divine direction" that would carry me down the road!

Soon I would be leaving on an amazing journey of hope and good will. The first day would take me only about 100 miles, where I would spend a night to work out any issues that I would have to address. Though I was unsure of what each day might bring, I did know that it would be a grand adventure!

My only apprehension was from an incident that had happened one week earlier. Since I had always been quite accident prone, I was not surprised when I zigged, instead of zagged, and hit my head on a metal beam in my garage. Since that day I had been experiencing short bouts of vertigo, which, at times, found me walking like a drunken sailor!

MOTORCYCLE SAFETY GEAR

¾ helmet with sun visor, face shield and vents;

Kevlar lined jeans padded at the knees, hips and buttocks, rated for 4 seconds of skid time;

Long and short sleeve wicking tee shirts;

Leather, ankle high, lace up, non-skid boots;

High visibility yellow, vented, jacket with shoulder, elbow and back armor;

Full rain gear with high visibility yellow, vest;

Leather gloves with padded knuckle and fingertips;

Extra thick, wicking, boot socks;

Magnetic, removable, tank bag;

Velcro attachable bra wallet;

Nylon, weather resistant luggage;

Camping equipment duffel bag;

Handle bar helmet lock;

Cruise control;

USB 12V charger outlet;

Engine guards with highway foot pegs;

Full windshield.

THE JOURNEY

Thursday, June 11th, 2015   Day 1

I left Venice, Florida at 9:00 am, and cruised onto the Interstate under an overcast sky with the threat of rain. After about 45 minutes, I pulled into a rest area to recheck my gear and make sure that the straps were still tight. All was well, and while preparing to continue on to my first destination, I was approached by an extremely friendly gentleman who was curious about my travels. He spoke broken English, though we did manage to share some experiences and a hug. By the way, hugs are the same in all languages!

A familiar family nudist resort in Lutz, Florida was my first stop for the night. Even, though, only 1 ½ hours from home, it would be the perfect place to do a shakedown to be sure that I had everything that I would need for a month of camping. I stayed there often, where all was familiar, so I could pick up anything that I needed before setting out on my long journey.

Upon my arrival, I waterproofed my tent with silicone spray, unpacked my gear and visited with old friends who were very excited to hear about my tour. Having known me for many years, they were not surprised by my quest and they openly shared their love and support. My "zany, creative buddy", was the first to donate to my cause. He never ceases to amaze me with his newest outlandish creations, to the chagrin of his neighbors! This sweet gentleman took it upon himself to encourage donations from "the maintenance man", "the lady on the lake", and "the flower lady." This was, truly, just the beginning of how numerous my "angels" would be, and the many roles that they would play along the way!

Later in the day, I was in the hot tub relaxing when I struck up a pleasant conversation with an interesting, older gentleman. I told him about my tour, and he spoke of his late wife and of his career. Now retired, and unfortunately a widower, he was troubled with what to do next. He seemed lonely and sad and admittedly craved friendship. I suggested that he buy a motorhome and see the country, meeting new friends along the way. I said: "life is short, so make of it what you can, while you can". I could only hope that I planted a positive seed of a brighter future for him. Later he stopped by my tent to tell me that I had "made his day" and that my story changed his attitude and his life forever! He then handed me a wad of bills to buy some gas for the trip, which would buy me a whole lot of miles! I felt totally blessed, indeed!

Early in the evening, I was relaxing and reading at the picnic table when friends stopped by and said that they wanted to take me out to dinner. We jumped into their golf cart and went up to the café by the pool. It was a beautiful night and we had fun visiting, the three of us and a friend of theirs. The veggie burger was tasty and the atmosphere was delightful as we ate together, outdoors, on red, gingham checked, covered tables, which reminded me of childhood picnics.

After our pleasant dinner, I laced up my ballet pointe shoes and joyfully danced on an open stage overlooking the lake, to my favorite classical music. It was a magical day and a great start to my trip!

I had such a nice time with so many of my friends. Nudists are wonderful people, so totally down to earth, and accepting of you exactly as you are, without judgment.

Obviously, once the clothes come off, we are all basically the same, just God's creations in our birthday suits!

At about 10:00 pm I crawled into my little green tent and read from "Walden" by Henry David Thoreau. I had totally devoured this book back in the 1980's when I was living aboard my 24 foot sailboat, "Whisper". I found it to be quite intriguing, so I kept it in my library for all of those years. I pulled it out for the trip, since I felt that it was quite appropriate, and once  again it was very inspiring! After just a short period of reading, I was off to sleep in my cozy little cocoon.

I rode 95 miles on this day.

Friday, June 12th, 2015   Day 2

I was up at the crack of dawn to pack my gear and get on the road for a lunch date with a high school friend that I had not seen in 42 years.

We were to meet at a restaurant on Interstate 75, at the Belleview, Florida exit. I knew her as soon as she got out of her car. She still had that same beautiful smile and sparkling personality! We had about a two hour chat and truly enjoyed our time together. We spoke of our friendship when we were quite young and naive. It was interesting  how much we learned about each other during our lunch, that we did not know while in school. I had always been so impressed with her amazing voice when we sang together in the school choir. She often had the lead solo, and deservedly so. Now she is married to a pastor and devotes her beautiful voice to the church choir. It was great to hear about her life with a wonderful husband, children, and many grand children! She presented me with an "angel" pin and a precious card with a poem called: "Angels Are Watching Over You". I thanked her for believing in me and my cause, and with a hug and a farewell, I was on the road again.

It was then that I realized, "this is it, and I am really doing it"! After months of planning, I was finally on my way! I would take Interstate 75, towards Ocala, Florida and then on to Perry, Florida where I would get onto HWY 27, otherwise known as the "Scenic Hometown Highway". I would take this all the way to Tennessee. Unfortunately, throughout the day, I was experiencing symptoms of vertigo as I traveled along winding, country roads.

I arrived at the Perry campground, at about time for the office to close, but the nice receptionist set me up with a site, complimentary of the owners. While pitching my tent, I met a couple who offered me some ice and a cold drink. I was also greeted by a very sweet calico kitty who hung around my campsite all evening, snuggling up and making me feel quite at home. A feline "angel", for sure!

Later, while in the shower room, I met a woman who was quite troubled. We shared life stories and she revealed the fact that she was in an abusive relationship that made her feel trapped. I encouraged her to find the strength to do whatever it took to find her way out. Though not obviously encouraged, she was still grateful for the friendship and understanding, and said that I was a great inspiration to her. She promised to stay in touch, and I hoped to hear from her soon.

It was just getting dark when the owner's young son came by to introduce himself. He said that his parents wanted him to check up on me to be sure that all was well. I was thankful for the sense of security and told him how impressed I was with his thoughtfulness and very polite demeanor. In these days when young people seem to lack integrity, I make an effort to praise those who strive to be better.

I went off to bed with more of Thoreau's teachings and eventually was lulled to sleep. Unfortunately, my sense of security vanished at about 2:45 am when I was stirred awake by a shadowy figure standing next to my tent. This man was inebriated and shouting profanities that described his intended actions. I froze and quickly realized that when I switched from my old tent to the new one, that I had purchased for the trip, I did not remember to transfer the large safety pins (my son's diaper pins from 1974) that I used to pin the zippers together for some sense of safety. This man could easily unzip the tent and get inside! I pulled my gun from its holster and then scrambled to find anything I could use to hook the zippers together. I found a small safety pin in my shower bag and a paper clip in my tank pouch. Then, I quickly secured both front and back panels and sat positioned to shoot if need be. I announced very loudly that I was armed and not afraid to use my weapon. He retreated and I never saw or heard from him again for the rest of the night. Negative thoughts challenged my positive outlook as I laid back down and ran through all of the nightmarish possibilities of what could have happened if my threat had not discouraged the intruder. I knew that I could not let this incident destroy all of the courage that I had summoned up to leave the safety of my home in order to set out on such a journey. I redirected my thoughts and, amazingly enough, fell back to sleep, after the adrenaline rush had subsided!

I rode 196 miles on this day.

Saturday, June 13th, 2015   Day 3

I was anxious to depart from the location of the previous night's disturbing fiasco, so I was up early and ready to go by 6:00 am. As most of my family and friends know, I do not drink alcohol. I have never had a problem with it, but I have had a lot of trouble with people that did. My past is riddled with bad experiences from those who indulged, and caused me undue grief through the outcome of their alcoholic behavior. I truly do not believe that drinking alcohol brings good to any situation, and now I had another perfect example to prove it. My peace of mind was, once again, compromised. I would now have another mental picture to add to my already troubling inventory of past encounters with totally irresponsible, and fully inebriated individuals.

I found out that the troubled lady I had met in the campground shower room was also the spouse of the drunken intruder! No wonder her frame of mind was so hopeless.

The next day I was headed for Georgia. I would take HWY 27/19 to Albany, then HWY 82 to Dawson, and HWY 280 to Columbus, Georgia. The weather was hot, but dry, and a beautiful day for a ride!

Before I left the town of Perry, Florida, I stopped at a shopping plaza and ran into my friend from the previous night's campground. She had abuse and desperation etched all over her face. Seeing her reminded me of the days when I suffered the same fate of emotional, verbal, and physical abuse, and made me thankful that those days had been over for me for a very long time. I now knew how I deserved to be treated and would not tolerate anything less. Once again, I encouraged her to find a way out of her difficult situation and she said that she was grateful for my strength and kindness. It is amazing how God will put us where he needs us, in order to share our experiences, when it may strengthen another in their time of need.

I picked up some hooks to secure the tent zippers and some more waterproofing spray for my camping gear. While checking out, the cashier asked me about the fact that I was carrying a motorcycle helmet and wanted to know what kind of bike I rode and where I was headed. I told her about my campaign tour and she expressed that I had encouraged her to get a bone density test as soon as possible. She was not aware that osteoporosis was a "silent killer". She gave me a big bear hug and then it was time to be on my way.

After several miles on the road, I was hot, thirsty, hungry, and tired so I stopped and parked at a grocery store lot in a very small town in Northern Florida. The area seemed a bit seedy, and I felt some apprehension, but it looked safe enough. I got under the shade of a tree and unpacked my lunch. Slowly a squad car drove by and continued to make several more passes. He did not approach me, so I felt that I was of no interest to him. After I had eaten, I knew that I needed a nap, so I made a pillow with my jacket, tucked my valuables and my firearm next to my body and fell off to sleep. When I awoke, there was "Mr. Policeman" parked close by and watching over me. As I repacked my gear, I thought about how one can't really know what danger they might put themselves in while traveling in such unknown localities. Being aware of the surroundings, when you are a woman alone, is extremely important. He was a guardian "angel" put into my path for protection.

You really cannot make a wrong turn. I thought that I did, and was frustrated with the delay, but when I turned around to get back onto the highway going north, I spotted a roadside vegetable stand. I had been looking forward to some fresh food, so I pulled over. After purchasing some cucumbers, peppers, and tomatoes, I began to ready my bike to leave when just then "Mr. Veggie" said: "Hey, you are the lady on the internet traveling across the country to promote the awareness of Osteoporosis and you are very famous!" Ha! Well, that was my 15 minutes of fame! He then handed me a donation for gas. So "angels" also grow gardens!

As I was coming into Columbus, Georgia, I began having flashbacks and felt as though I had been there before. Suddenly, I remembered that it was when my son, Anthony, graduated from Camp Bennington while in the National Guard. It was over 20 years ago, yet the memories came flooding back! Unfortunately, it was the last time that I had seen my eldest son before his tragic death, so it was quite bittersweet. I was blessed with two sons, though both had already passed. Anthony (Tony), ended his life at age 20, and Andrew (Andy), was a premature birth. I lingered alongside the road to absorb the experience and regain my composure. That was an unexpected, although cherished, moment.

Even though it had already been a long day, I felt the need to keep on riding, so I continued north to Pine Mountain, Georgia, where my partner recommended that I stay. He had been there before and said that I would find it to be quite a scenic ride. He was right. It was amazingly beautiful, with deep woods and winding roads!

When I got to the campground at Pine Mountain, the office was closed and there was no information available for tent camping. It was getting dusk and I knew that I could not go on any further, so I started down the road and followed a sign to the tent sites. All of a sudden the paved road turned into a very thick mix of sand, gravel and mud. It was too late to turn around, for the 100# of gear on the back of my bike made it impossible for me to navigate on the unstable surface. There was only one way out of my predicament, and that was straight down a very steep and slippery slope! It took all of my strength and I was terrified every inch of the way as I slowly crept, with what now felt like a much larger motorcycle under me, on down to the bottom of the hill. I prayed to God that I would make it safely and knew that if I got my bike and myself through this experience unscathed, that I was strong enough to take on any challenge that came my way. Well, after about an hour, I had done it, but not without expressing a few colorful words and coming very close to dropping my bike a half dozen times. With my brittle bones, a fall with my bike could have been tragic, even standing still! I was so thankful to have gotten through that dilemma unharmed and with my bike still in one piece. Exhausted and shaken, I pulled off to the side of the road and set up my tent, in the dark, on a very small section of grass. In the morning, the campground host gave me a 25% discount since I technically did not park in a paid space. Every little bit helps, but I would have paid them double to have not had that harrowing experience!

I rode 249 miles on this day.

Sunday, June 14th, 2015   Day 4

When I awoke, I was once again met with the familiar and unwelcomed dizziness of vertigo. Though I knew that it was dangerous to ride under such health conditions, I just could not imagine not continuing on with my tour. I had worked so hard with preparations and so many people had been cheering me on. So, fueled with determination, I left the campground at 10:00 am on my way to Chattanooga, Tennessee. I rode no more than 50 mile jaunts as not to run out of gas between towns. The Scenic Hometown Highway 27 route was exhilarating with all of its quaint little cottage homes and delicate summer flowers, filling up boxes and borders along the way. You definitely know that you are northbound when you see homes with basements and signs that say: "Bridges Ice Over Before Roadway"!

Sitting at a stoplight, I met a fellow biker who was from Virginia. He said that he had started out early on a Saturday morning to go for a ride and ended up in Mississippi! He was having so much fun that when he got on the road, he just kept on going. He was on his way home with a "lobster red" sunburn, as proof of his many days of exposure! I travelled with him for about 40 miles before we went our separate ways. Even a short stint of friendship can ward off the lonesome riding blues!

I planned on camping in Trenton, Georgia, just before the Tennessee border. All was well until I received some bad directions to a campground, and found myself lost on Lookout Mountain in Tennessee. It was a very treacherous ride up with 15 mph hairpin turns and steep grades. At the top of the mountain, I sat for about an hour trying to get a signal on my cell phone in order to consult my GPS for directions. The signal was poor, so it was to no avail. I was getting very nervous about being alone as darkness fell, without a soul or vehicle in sight. Finally, I saw a pickup truck coming up the road. The cab was occupied by two unsavory looking characters, and though against my better judgment, I flagged them down for help. The two men in the pickup truck said that they knew of a "short cut" to a campground back down the "other side of the mountain"! I thanked them both and took off as quickly as I could get my wheels turning before they were able to exit their vehicle. It seemed as if I had been on the road forever, when extremely fatigued, and having been lost for over two hours, I decided to stop and double check the directions with someone else who had pulled off the road. With a puzzled expression on their faces, they revealed that I had been directed the longest way around the mountain. I was actually only ten minutes away from the campground where I had asked for help! There was another long hour of twisted and jagged roadway before I finally reached my destination for the night. Once again, I arrived at the campground late and found the office closed. And, once again, I had to navigate more unstable ground. I felt like I was playing out a scene from "Twilight Zone"! I crept into the campground on loose gravel and parked my bike at the front of the office.

A nice young man noticed my dilemma and walked me around to find the closest and safest place to set up my tent, and a camper in a motorhome told me that it would be fine with him if I set up behind his unit on the lawn, which was very close to the front gate. This location had the least amount of gravel cover and would be easier for me to navigate on my way out, down another hill, in the morning. Within minutes, the office received a complaint from a nosy neighbor, that I was not camped in a designated spot. The owner showed up, and after hearing my plight, he gave me the campsite "on the house"! I thanked the campground host, profusely, for being so kind and understanding.

After a swim in the pool, to cool down and loosen up my sore muscles, I was able to relax and put the day and all of its challenges into perspective. My mother frequently said that things always look better in the morning, so I had high hopes that I might awaken to a more favorable day.

I crawled into my tent for a good night's sleep after strenuous hours of riding on treacherous mountain terrain with more than 600 pounds of my motorcycle and gear beneath me. It was then that I realized that even with all of the trials and tribulations, I was still there to tell about it!

I rode 185 miles on this day.

Monday, June 15th, 2015   Day 5

While packing up my gear in the morning, I became dizzy, slipped on the dew covered grass, and fell against a wooden picnic table, spraining my right wrist and little finger. This was just what I needed when it took so much strength just to stand my bike up, let alone handling it through such rough territory with an injured limb!

Upon leaving, I had to inch my bike carefully down the hill, and back through shifting gravel, until I was finally on solid pavement. I was off for another long day of twisting and winding roads, where I either had to navigate skillfully, or end up over a jagged cliff! I had traveled the Tennessee Mountains many times by car, but under these extreme conditions, a motorcycle, with so much added gear, was quite a different animal!

Halfway through the day, I realized that I had not eaten a hot meal since lunchtime on day two, so I stopped at a fast food restaurant for a hot baked potato and a veggie salad. Food never tasted so good. You can only eat so many nuts and berries!

It was another long day of riding with the Burkesville, Kentucky campground 30 miles out of the way and up another mountain. When I finally arrived, it was 6:30 pm. The pool was to close at 7:00, so I hurried down for a swim. As I floated leisurely in the pool, I took stock of the amazing experiences that I had already accumulated in just five days, and wondered about what other adventures might await me as I continued down the road.

Upon returning to my campsite, I noticed that the neighbors next to me had a unique, old, wooden boat sitting on a trailer. I admired the sleek lines as I took a quick stroll around it, relishing in my love for such classic vehicles of all kinds. After dinner, I knocked on their motorhome to beg a cup of ice. They were quick to oblige and then, having noticed that I had taken a keen interest, they invited me to have a closer look at their boat. We had a nice chat and then it was time to call it a day.

Unfortunately, I had to set up my tent on a downhill slope, so when I crawled into my sleeping bag I had to decide which way I should lie in hopes of not sliding down the hill! That night I relished in more spiritual philosophy from  Thoreau, and felt at peace as I fell asleep in my little abode.

I rode 215 miles on this day.

Tuesday, June 16th 2015   Day 6

Before leaving the campground, I saw my neighbor wave good bye to her husband as he drove off with his boat and trailer on a fishing excursion. She then walked over and invited me to join her for some morning juice and a gab session. We talked mostly about family, courage and independence, and also shared our personal views on the importance of balance for women in such challenging times. What a delightful and insightful lady that I had the good fortune to share the company of! The visit brought back memories of when I was very young and my mother would "coffee clutch" with the neighbor ladies. They drank coffee and ate "coffee cake", whilst spreading the latest gossip and discussing the ins and outs of family life. Now, unfortunately, social networking has eliminated those intimate gatherings.

One of the most important things about traveling safely on a motorcycle is the departure routine. Just as when I flew private airplanes, I made sure that I followed, very closely, my motorcycle "takeoff checklist". It would be so easy to leave something loose or unbuckled that could really ruin your day. So, with this, I was very diligent and methodical. "Murphy's Law" will get you if you are not paying attention!

I checked and rechecked my gear and then waved goodbye to my newfound kindred spirit. You never know when you will meet a person who will find their way into your heart and soul. This was one of those rare occasions. Interestingly enough, we will probably never see each other again, though I am sure that we planted some seeds that will grow and prosper long after our meeting.

Leaving the park, I recognized that all too familiar and dreaded noise of a loose chain. This could become a major catastrophe if the chain fell off, wrapping into the engine or locking up the back wheel. I pulled out my cell phone and did a search for the closest motorcycle shop. There was one in Glasgow, Kentucky, which was on route 90 W and only about 40 miles from my location. When I arrived at the dealership they took my bike inside, adjusted the chain and checked my tire pressure. I was in and out in about 15 minutes, free of charge! I was so very appreciative of them for getting me safely back on the road!

The sky was threatening rain all day and fortunately I found a gas station with a cafe' when the downpour came. As I pulled up for fuel, I became unsteady and fell with my bike up against the pumps. I was able to regain my balance enough to pull the bike back up, and though shaken, but no worse for wear, I

just staved off the adrenaline rush and went inside. There I found a quaint and charming little restaurant with blue gingham tablecloths and a wait staff who went out of their way to make me a hot bowl of bean soup and a plate of steamed vegetables. I was in heaven, totally dry and with my hunger satisfied, though quite troubled with having had another vertigo episode. I knew that I had to venture on, so after the rain stopped, I thanked the gracious café staff in Hodgenville, Kentucky and headed on down the road with a purpose and a positive attitude to carry me along. Once again, I had been blessed by unforeseen "angels".

I continued throughout the day, dodging three major rain storms, being chased by two vicious dogs and driving through a mud pit that covered me and my bike in a thick, mucky silt! With all of those close calls, and even more than I was willing to reveal, I was still having a wonderful time! After all, it was about the ride that was allowing me to share my knowledge across the country and the gift of strength and inspiration that I was receiving in return.

As I motored my bike along HWY 90 W, the sights were breathtaking. I would have loved someday to take my time traveling and photographing those amazing scenes with rustic red barns, majestic flowered cemeteries and rich, green, backyard gardens. They were very tantalizing to my creative eye!

I was approaching the Indiana border, when a "chopper" (a motorcycle with an extended front fork) with "ape hangers" (ridiculously angled handlebars) and a rider not wearing a helmet, came blowing past me. I barely caught the "colors" (the motorcycle club patch on his back) that the rider was "flying" (wearing). He was a member of the "Grim Reapers" (a rough motorcycle club). I thought to myself: "how appropriate with the reckless way that he was riding, speeding and risking his life!"

The tropical storm that came in from the Gulf of Mexico and had slammed Texas was also responsible for creating havoc in the Midwest, and I was headed straight into it! As I tried, but failed to outrun the storms, it was obvious to me that I would have to seek out a motel room for the night. I must admit that this idea was appealing, as I dreamed about the comfort of a cozy bed and a hot bath.

After checking into the motel in Huntingburg, Indiana, I began to unload my luggage into the room. When I set up at the campsites, I only removed the duffle bag that held the tent and cooking supplies. I was not concerned with removing my larger pack, since I always parked my bike close enough to my tent that I could hear if anyone attempted to tamper with it. As I tried to lift the heavier piece, I realized that my partner had helped me load it on my bike, and I was finding out that I was not strong enough to unload it! Frustrated and discouraged, I asked for help from a gentleman in the parking lot, knowing that I would have to brainstorm a system before my next motel lodging!

I was up to a bit of socializing, so I strolled down to the main lobby and started up a conversation with some of the other guests. Loneliness can get a grip on a solo traveler and I remedied this by making friends with strangers.

My muscles were beginning to feel the strain of six days, and over 1,000 miles on the bike, so I went back to the room looking forward to a relaxing bath. There wasn't a tub stopper anywhere to be found, so I inquired at the office. The desk clerk said that they no longer had any of them. Obviously they thought that they could save money by forcing their patrons to take a shower instead. I became creative and made a stopper out of a tin foil wrapper, from an energy bar, and had a nice long soak. I would find this to be a common problem along the way, since luxury is not to be found in low rent motels. Before going to bed, I took the time to fix a meal of ramen noodles, which I managed to cook in the microwave using the ice bucket. Challenges faced thus far made me appreciate these simple comforts even more.

Since I really couldn't afford the $99 room rate, I had a heart to heart conversation with the office desk clerk and was able to bargain her down to just $75. Though it would have been worth almost any expense, since a tremendous storm hit the area in the middle of the night! I wasn't experiencing much luck when it came to the weather, and I was finding out that the motel lodging was much too expensive for my budget, so I hoped that Mother Nature would cooperate with me in the future, that I might have the opportunity to do more tent camping along the way.

I rode 231 miles on this day.

Wednesday, June 17th, 2015   Day 7

After being on the road for a week, I was anxious to reach Merrillville, Indiana, where I would be staying with family for three days to visit, regroup and take a much needed rest.

Since Indiana was my home state, I felt a bit melancholy as I came up on the rambling fields of corn and soybeans. I remember the saying when I was young, that the corn should be "knee high by the 4th of July"! With flooding everywhere, the fields had just become overflowing lakes! There would not be any normal, healthy crops that season. I had never seen anything like it, before, in the 24 years that I had lived in the area.

As I passed through Jasper, Indiana, I wondered what the horrendous odor was that was drifting through the air. It was impossible to believe that anyone would choose to live there with such a horrible smell. It was then I realized that in front of the car ahead of me was a hog hauler. The stench was horrific! I felt so bad for all of the hogs with their noses pushing through the grates. I wanted to hijack the driver and set the poor little pigs free! That is one thing about riding on a motorcycle, you pick up on all of the available aromas, good or bad. This leaves the honeysuckle and fresh mown hay to be even more appealing!

I wanted to try and locate some very dear friends of mine in Lafayette, Indiana. We hadn't been in contact for at least ten years, so I was thrilled when the phone rang, and I heard a very familiar voice at the other end. We met for dinner, and while conversing over our meal, the strangest thing happened. I felt the sensation of fluttering wings in the sleeve of my jacket. Then, all of a sudden, out flew a butterfly! It landed on the floor beneath our table, so I got

down on my knees, scrambling around until I captured it. When I took it outside to set it free, it became obvious to me that my son, Tony, was also partaking in this journey. Some "angels" can fly on butterfly wings!

I was in my backyard gardening on that fateful morning when I received the call that my son, Tony, had passed. Hysterical and reeling in shock, I felt my heart breaking. Just then a butterfly landed on my forehead. After shooing it away, it came back and rested on my shoulder, where it stayed for an indefinite amount of time. I had heard stories in the past of how butterflies are a sign of our loved ones, who are no longer with us, making contact to console our grief. So I knew for that precious time that he was still with me.

One of the most interesting discoveries on this tour were the windmills. I came upon a field of more than one hundred of them. It was very surreal since the storms were whipping up the wind and spinning them wildly, bright white against a deep, ultramarine blue, clouded, sky. They seemed almost terrestrial in nature, as they generated a lot of power on that day!

My son, Tony, was buried in the town of Rensselaer, Indiana, which was along my mapped out route, so I rode hard all day, through the rain, in an attempt to get to the cemetery before dark. When I got near, all three entrances were flooded and blocked off with barricades. I decided to do what I had to in order to get past them, since I knew that I could not allow myself to be defeated, without making a gallant effort. I summoned up the confidence that I needed for the challenge, revved up my engine, and rode through the least threatening of the water troughs. Thank goodness that I was going at a high rate of speed since the water came up to my knees and washed over the gas tank of the bike! At this point, I still could not  proceed further, so, though forlorn, I realized that I would not be able to visit my son's grave on that evening. The disappointment was crushing. Trips to my home state were few and far between, and even though I know that only my son's physical remains are there, and spiritually he is with me always, it is still consoling to visit where he was laid to rest. In the end, I felt quite fortunate to have travelled the last 50 miles safely to that location.

I planned to stay at my niece's new home, and since I had never been there before, upon arrival I was dismayed when I found that her garage, where I was to park my motorcycle, was up a long driveway with a severely steep incline. Just another mountain to climb!

After a pleasant visit with family, I soaked in the tub and climbed into a warm bed.

I rode 257 miles on this day.

Thursday, June 18th, 2015   Day 8

I woke up feeling exhausted, but refreshed. In 7 days I had travelled 1,400 miles. Not a small feat for a 60 year old, 5 foot 4 inch, 100 pound, petite woman riding a 500 pound motorcycle with 100 pounds of gear!

After having breakfast with my family, they went off to work, with plans for us to meet for dinner later in the evening. I spent the rest of the morning doing laundry, drying out my packs, and catching up on my journal.

In the afternoon, I was attacked by an unleashed dog. It was of the Chow breed, which are commonly known to be unpredictable. Ironically, I came all of the way unscathed, only to get bit by a dog, and I wasn't even on the bike! I spent three hours at the local clinic having an x-ray of my elbow, irrigating the wound, bandaging it and receiving a prescription for an antibiotic. The doctor also gave me a brace to wear when riding until it was totally healed, since the puncture went into the muscle. I was extremely thankful that the incident did not alter my trip in any way.

That evening my family took me out to dinner and to a concert in the park. The music was rock and roll, so I did enjoy the opportunity to shake my booty just a bit! While on the dance floor, I was approached by a high school friend who had read about my tour on a social media site. It was wonderful to relive some of my youthful past as we shared memories together. At any time we can climb into a time machine and be transported back to our age of innocence!

No miles were ridden on this day.

Friday, June 19th, 2015 Day 9

While getting ready for the day, I was hit with one of the worst vertigo attacks since leaving home. I found myself braced up against the bathroom sink and holding onto the doorknob as the room spun around me. It felt like when I was a child, back on the playground, spinning on a merry-go-round out of control. Slowly, I collapsed to my knees and clung to the floor while I cried out for help. Fortunately, family was within earshot and they were able to assist me. Fear, once again, began to creep in and take hold of me. I questioned my ability to continue riding under such dire circumstances, though I knew that I had to count on my inner drive and determination to carry me through.

I chose to spend the rest of the day with my feet planted firmly on the ground, so I sat for hours on a low stool,  cleaning my bike after its mud bath from two days of traveling in the rain. Every nook and cranny were spotlessly clean when I had finished. I have often been accused of being obsessive about maintaining my motorcycle, but I always fall back on the saying that "Cleanliness is next to Godliness"! I have also found that you cannot really know, or understand, the function of a vehicle until you get down and personal with the maintenance of its operating parts!

My family made special plans to take me to an evening art walk in a neighboring town, and even though I felt appreciative, and did not want to disappointment them, I opted for some rest and quiet time alone. Suffering from sore muscles and extreme fatigue, I knew that I would not be good company. I cooked a healthy dinner, and then after taking a spa bath, I laid down in bed to continue reading from "Walden". Since I have always been a loner and quite philosophical, I could easily relate to Henry David Thoreau's masterpiece.

No miles were ridden on this day.

Saturday, June 20th, 2015   Day 10

I decided to take a short trip on my bike to De Motte, Indiana to visit my niece who lives there. I surprised her with my arrival, and caught her still in bed. She threw on a robe, stepped into her slippers, and welcomed me to join her for a chat on the patio. She spoke of her children and the uphill challenges of raising them, alone. I have often reminded her of our Sullivan bloodline and how courage and strength just flows through our veins. We then talked about our life in general and of our hopes and plans for the future. With hugs and wishes of good will, I was, once again, on my way. I rode back to Merrillville, where I attended the memorial of a cousin who had passed months previous. It was nice to see family members that I had lost track of over the years and to share in the memory of our late family member. When the podium was open to share our past experiences with him, I told of when I was 17 years old and had shown up at a party that he was also attending. He was older than I and took the role of protector as he quickly ushered me out the door, saying that it was not a place where I belonged. I always respected him for that. He used to call me his "cool little cousin".

After paying my respects, I met up with my immediate family for a small get together where I was able to spend time with some of my great-nieces. I have missed out on the joy of watching them grow, living so far away, so those were moments to cherish. When I rode back to where I was staying, it began to rain just as I pulled my bike into the garage. I

was happy to have stayed dry, and felt blessed that I did not have to wipe down the whole bike, once again!

Depending on weather the next day, I had planned to continue my journey to the west coast of Michigan and then on to its upper peninsula. I was anxious to move towards my goal and looked forward to what lay ahead. I prayed for safe travel and blessings along the way.

I rode 53 miles on this day.

Sunday, June 21st, 2015   Day 11

I left my niece's home in Indiana at about 11:30 am, on my way to Northern Michigan. I was thankful to all of my family for their hospitality and for allowing me a much needed rest at that point of my journey. I really enjoyed my

beautiful great-nieces. They are so very adorable and intelligent just like their "Crazy Aunt Nancy"! My honorable title comes from when my nephew was only four years old and I had telephoned their home. When he picked up the phone, I asked to speak to his daddy. He dropped the receiver, and as it clattered to the floor, I heard him in the background yelling to his dad: "Crazy Aunt Nancy is on the phone!" From the mouth of babes.

After riding only about a mile, the strap on my duffle bag broke and it nearly fell off of the luggage rack before I was able to pull over. I found myself on the side of the road, next to a barbeque stand, where the proprietor supplied me with some tools so that I could try to reshape the hook that had come apart. The connection was beyond repair, so I called out to a farmer from across the road to see if he might have some bailing wire to get me through until I could get to a hardware store. He jumped down off of his tractor and headed for the barn. Upon his return, he provided me with a sturdy ratcheting strap, which I later sent back to him along with a thank you note, once I got home. Just some good old "Hoosier Hospitality" and I was back on the road. Those country "angels" saved the day!

I took Route 2 to La Porte, Indiana, and had stopped for gas when a customer there shared some local knowledge of a pleasant bike ride around the lake, which would also allow me to avoid the busy interstate. It was a bit out of the way, but well worth the view!

At 3:00 pm I crossed the state line into Michigan and began to suspect more chain issues. I pulled off into a rest  area to take a look and found that it was definitely loose again! Just then a man walked by wearing a tee shirt with a motorcycle logo on it. I asked him if he knew of a place where I could get my chain tightened and he said "let's just do it here!" I was game, so I got out my tools and we went to work. Another guy also stopped by and offered the perfect sized wrench that we needed to get the job done. I was taught exactly what to do if I had to fix it, again, in the future. Both of those road "angels" resided in Grand Rapids, Michigan.

As I rode off, I couldn't help but to feel totally blessed with the "angels" that had shown up on this journey. Some of them were in human form and some of them allowed me to feel their presence with a cool chill from their fluttering, invisible, angelic wings.

At 5:00 pm, I saw a camping sign just off of the interstate in Coloma, Michigan. I immediately pulled onto the ramp since I did not want to find myself at dusk setting up camp as I had, unfortunately, done so far for most of the trip. The campground owners supported my cause by gifting me with a complimentary site. Blessed again! After unloading all of my gear, I went to the pool and hot tub where I met three generations of ladies. I enjoyed them tremendously as we shared girl talk and gossip! On the way back to my site, the vertigo reared its ugly head, again. I was tipping to one side with the whole world swirling around me, as I cautiously maneuvered back to my tent. I knew that there wasn't anything that I could do about it, so I decided that I would just have to soldier on!

The temperature had dropped to 66 degrees by the time that I tucked in, but my sleeping bag was warm and I slept snug all night!

I rode 99 miles on this day.

Monday, June 22nd, 2015   Day 12

Early in the morning, I headed to the ladies room where I washed up and began a conversation with another camper who spent most of her weekends camping there. She filled me in on some local knowledge of the area and then we began to connect on a much deeper level as I spoke of my quest. Once she found out that I was an artist and dancer, she shared her lifelong struggle to pursue her creative talent in art and dance. I encouraged her to "color outside the lines" and "dance like no one was watching". We also shared our thoughts on confidence and independence and how women are often challenged as they try to acquire those attributes. She had been married to an apathetic, controlling, and abusive husband, for many years, and sought an opportunity to leave him. I could only hope that this wonderful free spirit might someday be able to break the emotional chains that had bound her for so long.

In my travels I have found it to be the case that too many women stay in situations of control by a man. Once while traveling across the country in my motorhome, I was pulling into a campsite when I noticed several women sitting at a picnic table next to where I was to park. While backing up my 55 foot unit (a 32 foot class C with a 23 foot car hauler), I saw an expression of shock on their faces. As I stepped down out of my motorhome, they approached and asked how I could possibly have the courage to travel the country in such a large rig. I said to them: "It only takes two arms, two legs, two hands, two feet and a brain. The only body part that your husbands have that you don't is a penis, and it is of no use when driving a rig!" The women blushed bright red and I thought that they would just split a gut with laughter! They all agreed that there could be some changes coming along in their very near futures, when it came to the relationships with their partners. One of them even said that she was going to look into buying a motorhome and setting out on her own! It has always surprised me how some women have been brainwashed to believe that they are not capable of the same independence available to men, and that they would stay in unhappy unions in order to enjoy a lifestyle that they felt could only be given to them by the so called "stronger sex".

After leaving Coloma, Michigan at 11:00 am, I drove 12 miles up HWY 196 to South Haven, Michigan. As I came into town, I saw a library displaying a sign that said "Tourist Information". I thought that it was perfect timing since I would be able to get directions to the historic lighthouse there and do my computer update at the same time. It had been clouding over, so once inside, I asked about the local weather report. The librarian said that strong storms were predicted, but not until 3:00 in the afternoon. I sat down at the computer, believing that I had time to spare, with the intention of being back on the highway heading north before they hit. Within the hour there was a downpour! I continued with my computer work in hopes of waiting out the storm, but it was unrelenting. The librarians were very helpful pointing out directions to a motel that would see me through the night, though I would have to drive two miles in a deluge of rain. Because I could not see well in the storm, I passed it up and went three miles out of my way. I had to turn around on a slippery, wet, and narrow gravel shoulder. This had been my ongoing challenge throughout the trip, dealing with the weight of my bike and my lack of strength on rough terrain. Though I knew that I had the stamina and determination to get my bike and myself home safely, it seemed that I would also need to gather up some herculean strength to accomplish the task! So, drenched, cold, and thoroughly exhausted, "I pulled up my bootstraps" and continued on.

In the parking lot of the motel I was confronted, again, with the problem of my heavy pack. I figured out that if I got one shoulder under it, while wiggling it back and forth, I could slowly inch it off of the back rest and on to the seat. I was then able to scoot it, with my boot, into the room. Once all of my luggage was unloaded, I hung my clothes over the room heater and took a short nap. Upon waking, I called my partner to update my location and then addressed my replies to the phone calls, texts and emails from concerned and interested supporters of my tour. I decided to take a swim in the pool and do a workout at the gym, but, very quickly, I realized that the motel's "Health Club" was not only too isolated for my safety, and too filthy for my health, but also a gathering place for people of a much lower standard than I would choose to associate with. So I went back to the room to read and catch up on my journal. I was finding that I did not feel safe at the low rent motels even after I turned the lock on the room door!

There were more storms predicted to hit at around 9:00 pm, so I turned on the television and got an updated report. Very violent weather was on the way with 3 inches of rain, 60 mile per hour winds, golf ball sized hail and the threat of tornadoes. I decided that I had to try to protect my bike, so I turned it around, faced the windshield into the wind, backed it up tightly against the building, and tucked it under an awning. At that point, I had done all that I could do to prepare for what was to come. For the next few hours I stayed busy planning my route for the next day and preparing my dinner of beans and vegetables. Then I settled in with my book and tried to relax.

At 10:00 pm a tornado watch was in effect and quickly thereafter it was upgraded to a warning. Then the local weather station announced that it was heading right for the area where I was staying! I made several calls to my partner with continuous updates and information. I had never been in an extreme weather situation such as this while traveling on my motorcycle, so it was nice to feel as though I was not totally alone. By midnight the threat was over and I phoned to reassure him that all was well. We talked about the day that I had been through and the hope that I would have a better day to come. We said our goodnights and I fell off into a peaceful sleep.

I rode 33 miles on this day.

Tuesday, June 23rd, 2015   Day 13

After a very long and scary night in a nasty motel, with tornado warnings and treacherous weather, I was ready to leave South Haven, Michigan. It was a chilly morning with a temperature of 60 degrees and high winds. My plan for the day had been to do a watercolor of the South Haven lighthouse (only the first of all the lighthouses that I hoped to paint along the Michigan coast), but the winds were so strong that I could not even hold my camera still enough to get a decent photograph, let alone try to paint! Even though the Michiganders were enjoying the beach in bikinis, I had on several layers of clothing and was still cold! I decided that the weather was not appropriate for creating artwork and continued on.

In town, I found a natural food store where I was able to purchase some healthy treats. While sharing my story with the proprietor, a woman standing behind me joined in the conversation and spoke of her mother's and her own Osteoporosis issues. She had broken bones in her feet on several occasions, suffering terribly from the disease. She asked for my card and website information and then she handed me a cash donation. This was a generous gesture and it really touched my heart. I knew then and there, that my mission was not in vain.

While sitting on a park bench outside of the store and enjoying some amazingly tasty ginger cookies, I met a boy who was approximately seven years old. He was extremely interested in my cause. After asking many questions, he looked up at me with compassion and concern on his sweet face and said: "I hope you get better". My heart was truly melted by this little "angel"!

The next destination for that afternoon was Holland, Michigan, but when I saw the exit for Saugatuck, out of curiosity, I pulled off onto the ramp. What a quaint and beautiful setting! I loved the feel of that town. It was post card perfect! Unfortunately, I did not see their lighthouse, for it was over the dunes and I could not get close enough with the bike.

Later, while walking through the city park, I visited with a very fit, older gentleman who took his daily run there because he loved watching the ducks and taking in the splendid scenery. I also chatted with two ladies who were resting on a bench along the waterside. I was amazed when I found out that they were from my neighboring town of Port Charlotte, Florida. It is a small world!

While exploring the downtown area, I came upon an artist co-op. The thought crossed my mind to find some sort of trinket in remembrance of my trip, and in turn support the local artists, so I went inside. While I shopped, the owner and I had a wonderful interaction sharing hope and good news. I picked up a gorgeous, heart shaped, beach glass pendant, and as I admired it, she said: "Keep it for good luck!" She shared the fact that she had just created the piece for her shop, though wanted me to have it. Some people are creative "angels" in disguise!

I left the town of Saugatuck, Michigan with a sense of peace and serenity and thankful that I had not missed the opportunity to experience it.

My next stop was Holland, Michigan. Upon arriving, I headed straight for the state park. The ranger gave me an auxiliary campsite for only $15 which was a great deal. Most sites were costing up to $40 per night! I had no hookups or a picnic table, but I was happy to have landed safe and sound, if even with just the bare essentials of grass and sky! Immediately after setting up, I met a camping neighbor. He was a very pleasant gentleman who was concerned for my welfare while staying in a small tent. The temperature was supposed to drop down to 50 degrees that night and before settling into my bed, his sweet wife brought me a quilt to put over my sleeping bag. That quilt made a huge difference in my tent and in my heart! I slept cozy and warm that night knowing that there are thoughtful "angels" among us.

I rode 28 miles on this day.

Wednesday, June 24th, 2015   Day 14

I felt rested and refreshed, upon waking, so I decided to take a walk to the beach about two miles away to plan out my painting of the local lighthouse.

The sights were breathtaking as I passed many quaint cottages along the road and traditional sailboats at the marina. After returning to my campsite, and while packing up, I spoke with several people about my tour. A young woman took a great interest in my cause and thanked me for bringing an awareness to her about Osteoporosis. She was only in her early twenties and had no idea of how it could affect her life as she grew older.

Upon attempting to return the borrowed quilt to my campground friends, I realized that they had left for the day while I was off walking. I placed the quilt on their picnic table and as I continued to pack, I noticed that there was something on the seat of my motorcycle. Before she left, my neighbor had gifted me with her "daily devotional" and had attached a note that said she was praying for my safety. Such random acts of kindness can make a huge difference in the world!

As I was departing, I met up with the Children's Activity Coordinator for the park who was an amazing and enthusiastic young woman. She was as inspired by me and my journey, as I was by her beautiful spirit!

When I got back to the lighthouse, I found that the parking spaces only offered a two hour stay. The time limit made it totally impossible to finish a complete painting, though I was able to sketch up a pretty good rendition of Holland's "Big Red" that I would finish, later, back in my home studio. As I worked, I enjoyed visiting with several people, who stopped to comment on my artistic talents. It was quite an enjoyable experience that made me long for more time in that magical setting.

Traveling down HWY 31, my next stop was Grand Haven, Michigan. I had a very tasty black bean burger at the local grill and then drove off to search for the town's lighthouse. Once there, I found that there was a long line to get into the park. With a day use permit required, and since it was getting late, I decided to try to make it to Traverse City, Michigan, before dark. I knew that it could be a challenge because I would be pushing myself hard, on low energy and in cold weather, but I set out with a "can do" attitude and went on down the road.

The scenery was spectacular with rolling hills, farms and livestock. Fortunately, the weather was dry, but there was quite a bitter nip in the air. At about 60 miles from my destination, I pulled off for gas. Since the temperature was dropping further, and night was approaching, I inquired about lodging from a local resident. He said that he knew of a clean and reasonable motel in Traverse City, and that he would call the owner, who was a friend of his, to secure me a room. Leaving the gas station, I thought about how often "angels" appeared to meet my every need! As the sun set on the horizon, I was totally miserable from the cold, and thought that I would freeze to death! Yet, I carried on as I counted the long miles to my destination for the night. Upon my approach, I was so chilled that I could no longer feel my hands or feet. The owner of the inn was expecting me, and along with my room key, he graciously supplied me with fresh towels for cleaning my bike. He was also a motorcycle enthusiast and knew the major importance of maintenance while on the road. I was very thankful for his hospitality, and even more so for my room as I entered it and turned up the heat! Though I was just about starved, it was already 10:30 pm so I made myself a light dinner of almonds and raisins and went straight to bed. I fell off to sleep thinking of how much resolve I had acquired and of what an amazing day it had been.

I rode 217 miles on this day.

Thursday, June 25th, 2015   Day 15

In the morning, while polishing my bike, I spoke with the owner of the motel and he recommended that I visit the

"Old Mission Light" just outside of Traverse City. He said that it was located 17 miles down HWY M 37 and that it was a spectacular ride. As I cruised past scenic bays and farms, along with wineries and cherry groves, I was surprised by the rich and diverse agriculture that belonged to the state of Michigan.

Pulling into the parking area of the lighthouse, I noticed another motorcycle with a packed luggage rack and hoped that I might get a chance to visit with the traveling biker. Once inside, I knew immediately who the biker was. We all have that "look" when adorned in full riding safety attire. He also noticed me and we immediately struck up a friendly conversation. He and his wife were from Oklahoma and they had just vacationed together for a week riding along the Michigan coast. She had flown home ahead of him and he was completing a 5,000 mile trip, solo. After exchanging some of our personal motorcycle stories, we went our separate ways. As I finished my tour of the light tower, the keeper's quarters and the grounds, I contemplated on how much I had enjoyed the exchange of adventures with another kindred motorcycle spirit!

My favorite part of that sightseeing experience was the history of the woman who had been the tender of the light for many years back in the 1800's. Another courageous woman after my own independent and adventurous heart!

When I got back to the parking lot my motorcycle would not start. My heart just sank as I thought of how I was far too many miles away from help for a break down there. I had tried everything that I could think of, and then with one more push of the starter button, a miracle happened, and it just kicked over! I was unsure of the problem, but my gut told me that it would probably come back to haunt me in the near future. Though with this little scare, I had found out that "angels" were also motorcycle mechanics!

On the way back into Traverse City I pulled off at a scenic overlook. It was there that I met a young woman who was participating in a "Geo Caching" event. This is an Internet adventure where you travel to mapped out locations in hunt for treasure that has been buried there by previous participants. I joined her in the search, but to no avail. We believed that the prize was buried under a loose post, but even together we were not strong enough to pull it out of the ground. After a lot of effort, we finally gave up and said our good byes. I thought that I might like to try my hand at that unique adventure upon my return home.

Back on HWY31, in Traverse City, I topped off my gas tank and stopped at a drug store to speak with a pharmacist about the vertigo episodes that I had been experiencing. They began five days before departing on my journey, but I did not want to alarm friends or family, so I had kept it mostly "under hat". Since the symptoms had become more intense and longer in duration, I knew that it was time to address the problem. The consultation revealed that there was little that could be done about my dizziness, until I could see a doctor, except to take motion sickness drugs. I had already tried them, resulting in no relief. Instead, they had brought on severe drowsiness that almost resulted in a crash on a mountain in Tennessee! The issue had become quite challenging, to say the least, let alone the extreme danger of riding a motorcycle with dizzying sensations! I had a snack while resting on my bike and then waited out another vertigo spin before cautiously moving on down the highway.

After riding another ten miles, I spotted the gentleman from Oklahoma pulling onto the highway from a roadside restaurant. I honked and he waved and before long he was riding along side of me. At the next light he asked me what my destination was for that day. I told him about my plan to make it to the Mackinaw Bridge that night by way of Charlevoix and Petoskey, Michigan. He said that it would be a stretch, but he was also going that way and would ride along to help me accomplish my goal. He also said that when he left me back at the lighthouse he had regretted not mentioning to me that I should check out the "Mushroom Houses" in Charlevoix. Once we reached the downtown

area, I followed my friend as he wove in and out of traffic and up and down sloping streets past every one of them! They were so quaint and enchanting, as if they had come right out of a children's story book fairy tale!

I wanted to stop for lunch and he had friends to visit, so we parted with plans to meet up later in the afternoon. I ate an "Arizona Salad" at a local pub and then took a stroll down by the water. Clouds were forming in the west, so I pulled out my rain gear and suited up. I called my friend and then met him on my way out of town, headed for Petoskey. The rain hit half way there so we had quite a wet and chilly ride. On hilly terrain, with wet pavement, it was a struggle for me to hold up the weight of the bike. I was thankful that he knew his way around so that I could just follow him and keep my focus on the road. I had become weak and shaky, unsure if it was an adrenalin rush from the fear of dropping my bike, or just from being wet and cold to the bone, or both!

I felt that I needed a break before going on, so upon reaching Petoskey we found a health food store where we stocked up on groceries and rested with a snack and my favorite herbal drink. This also gave us some time to chat and share some more of our motorcycling experiences of the past, since both of us had been riding motorcycles most of our adult life. Before departing, we raised our glasses and gave a toast to safe travels ahead.

Our next stop was to be the Mackinaw Bridge. Sensing my excitement of reaching the halfway point of my tour, my friend said that though we would be going across the bridge later than planned, he would be happy to continue on along with me. It was obvious that I was on a mission, and that there would be no stopping me from making my destination on that night. While riding, he came up with the idea to document my crossing with a photo in front of the bridge, so we stopped in Mackinac City to do a  shoot. By 8:00 pm I was crossing the infamous span of the Mackinaw Bridge. It was so glorious with the setting sun and an awesome view. From the top of my lungs I shouted: "it's not over 'till it's over!" I was also giving thanks for another road "angel" who helped me to accomplish my goal by escorting me to my destination.

Once across the bridge and in the town of St. Ignace, we both realized that lodging was going to be a problem. There was a car show going on and the streets were packed. Without available campgrounds and each motel lighting up their "no vacancy" signs we had made the decision to cross back over the bridge and search elsewhere. It was then that he spotted one sign that said "vacancy". Much relieved, we hustled into the office with high hopes of procuring our rooms for the night. When the manager greeted us at the counter he said that they had a clean, comfy, queen size bed available for us. My friend grinned and said: "I don't think that my wife or her boyfriend would appreciate us getting a room together!" We all had a good laugh and then were given the keys to two separate rooms. Once unpacked, we rode our bikes to a restaurant in town, where we celebrated our journey with a hot meal. Back at the motel, we tucked our bikes in for the night and went off to our single rooms for a well-deserved night's rest.

It was an awesome day driven by strength, courage and determination, but also sweetened by friendship. It would be etched in my memory forever!

I rode 154 miles on this day.

Friday, June 26th, 2015   Day 16

I was out in front of the motel packing up my bike when I saw my motorcycle buddy coming back from breakfast. We took a selfie in the parking lot and said our farewells. He

was taking the northern route through Wisconsin and I was navigating south through the center of Michigan.

Before leaving St. Ignace, I had decided to take a stroll around town to see if I could find a unique souvenir that would represent the summation of the courage that it took for me to reach my destination. What I found was a miniature painting of the Mackinaw Bridge in a $15 charm that I hooked on my motorcycle key chain. It was the perfect form of memorabilia and it was also a rendition painted by a local artist. Even something so small would carry with it a meaning to be cherished for years to come!

The trip across the bridge at 10:00 am would turn out to be quite a different experience from the night before. There was a long line of waiting cars that were just inching along. Once again, this would be a difficult task for me. I was moving in slow motion with all of the extra gear weight. I held my bike steady as I crept forward until I was through the morning traffic congestion.

Several people had mentioned to me that I should not miss the "Tunnel of Trees" experience, so I rode off to find it. What I failed to know was that it would turn out to be 40 miles of extremely exhausting twists and turns that would take me along Lake Michigan's coastline. Though the views were spectacular, I experienced white knuckling fear as I navigated each bend in the road while trying to maintain the strength to keep on going. It seemed as though the road would never end, but I came to the point where I knew that for me there was no turning back. Just as in life, day by day, and mile by mile, we must go on. That amazing highway was beautiful, and ethereal in a sense, as it felt as though it had been placed there just for me as another challenge that I was destined to conquer!

I crossed the path of 52 bikers coming from the opposite direction. I know the exact number of bikes because I had pulled off of the road to rest and I counted every one! I also spotted a black squirrel and remembered them from when I was a child vacationing up in Michigan. They are a much larger species and do not in any way resemble the squirrels that I have at home in my yard! "No, Dorothy, you are not in Kansas anymore!"

When the Tunnel of Trees came to an end, I was extremely relieved, and found myself in the quaint and affluent town of Harbor Springs. I had lunch at a sidewalk cafe and truly enjoyed the "Vegan Delight" wrap sandwich. Afterwards, I took some time to unwind from such a challenging and exhausting ride and then distributed cards and bumper stickers along the street. It was then that I met a delightful, loving, and generous couple from Mississippi. They prayed for my safety and gifted me with a nice cash donation. We had a wonderful visit and then I was on my way to the next stop, which would be Houghton Lake, Michigan. This had not been a part of my trip plan, though once I had reached the state of Michigan, I was struck by a flow of memories that I needed to address.

For many years, during my childhood, my family had taken summer vacations at Houghton Lake. I had not been back there since. Now, 45 years later, I was not even sure that I could find my way. I would be seeking closure from an incident that I had experienced there when I was 10 years old and this was an opportunity to hopefully resolve some of those painful emotions.

Traveling on the interstate would be the fastest route to this destination, so I changed my itinerary from the back roads to highway and continued on. Soon I approached a sign that showed Houghton Lake having two separate exits. The first one said Higgins Road, and I remembered that it circled Higgins Lake, taking me several miles out of my way, so I rode further on until I was concerned that I had passed up the second exit. I was feeling disappointed, though also a bit relieved. I was unsure of my reaction, returning to a place that held such bittersweet memories. Just then, the exit that I thought I had missed was in sight. I quickly headed down the ramp and knew immediately that I was on the correct route. The smell of wood smoke wafting across the lake from fireplace chimneys brought back memories of the cool summers that I had spent there. How could I possibly find a resort that I heard had long since been sold and made into a condo association? Would the original name of it even exist? The only landmark in my memory was a gift shop that sat directly across the street. Could it still be there 45 years later? I stopped for fuel and asked a woman at the gas station about the resort and the gift shop. She

 thought the resort was no longer there, but she said that the gift shop was just a mile up the road. I was so excited that I had found my way back to the past, and to a place that I needed to make amends with!

As soon as I saw the gift shop on the side of the highway, many old memories tugged at my emotions. Then right across the road, was the resort. I pulled up to the old, log  cabin, "The Babe", and I could barely believe that it looked just like It had many years ago. Tears flooded my eyes as I climbed off of the bike to take a much closer look. That summer, when my precious innocence was stolen, had changed my life forever and there was my chance to get the closure that I had so long awaited. Just as I began to sob, uncontrollably, a lady rounded the corner of the cabin and asked if I was ok and if she could be of any help. My emotions erupted as she put an arm around me and listened to my story of how I had arrived and my need to experience a release from the past. Very lovingly she then said: "Well, let's just make this trip a positive experience that you can take home with you!" We took a tour of the resort and I was amazed that not one thing had changed. Even the old swing set was still in place! The new owners had done an amazing job of keeping history intact. There was a sunset party going on at the dock, so we joined in and I was introduced, all  around, to her friendly neighbors, who were also the joint owners of the resort. I reminisced of how I had fished and swam there as a child and how magical it had been to dangle my feet in the water on warm summer nights. Later, we walked to a quaint, local restaurant where I was treated to dinner. Once back at the resort, friends gathered closely around a campfire sharing the many memories of their experiences at Houghton Lake. It was quite rewarding when I was able to give back by offering up my stories of the past, as I remembered them.

Once the campfire embers cooled and everyone had dispersed, I was invited back to my new friend's home on the lake where she, her husband and I, visited until 10:00 pm. It was then that I realized I had not made any plans for lodging and asked their advice on finding a campground or motel for the night. They both looked at each other, shook their heads and said that I would be staying with them. It was a melancholy experience, for I had stayed in that very home during visits to the lake when my girlfriend's parents owned it. They put me up in the same room that I had shared with my friend. I laid down in that bed with a heating blanket and a fluffy pillow, safe and sound, and had a very peaceful night's rest. They were healing "angels" of mercy!

I rode 177 miles on this day.

Saturday, June 27th, 2015   Day 17

    It was a very chilly morning in Houghton Lake, Michigan, when my wonderful new friend and I sat together in front of a picture window overlooking the lake, and reminisced of the good times that cancelled out the bad experiences. It was very healing for me and I was truly thankful for her compassionate insight.

    Her husband joined us with an atlas of the United States and together we mapped out the part of my journey that would take me as far as North Carolina. They had recently come up from the south and knew which roads would be best traveled.

    I needed to have some work done on my bike at the local motorcycle dealership, which was located across the road from my friend's home. I rode over on my bike, while she followed me in her car. I had to purchase a new chain, since mine was loose, once again, and also in disrepair. They did not have one in stock, but located one in Flint, Michigan, which would become my next destination.

    We walked over to the gift shop to buy a few souvenirs, since as a child it was always something that I had looked forward to while on vacation at the lake. I was amazed that it had remained as I remembered it from years ago. It was like time had just stood still!

    I was packing up my bike for the next leg of my trip when I noticed that a small group of neighbors were approaching. They gathered around with hugs and well wishes, along with a large cash donation for my journey. I was so touched by their generosity and show of support that I could hardly speak. I said my good byes and rode on, a different person from whence I came.

It was a miserable, cold, wet and windy ride on to Flint, Michigan. When I reached the motorcycle repair shop the service manager was efficient and caring as he immediately checked in my bike. Then he escorted me over to a parking lot diner where I was able to warm up and enjoy some much needed sustenance. It was an old style café that was designed with a 1950's motif.

While enjoying my lunch, I met up with a Christian motorcycle fellowship. They had commented on how impressed they were with my mission and then picked up the tab and said prayers for my safety along the way. They were "angels", whose gesture had sweetened the day!

When I returned to the shop to pick up my bike, I noticed that the service manager had posted my Face The Fear Tour bumper sticker, that I had given him, on the back of the cash register for everyone to see! The support was endearing.

By the time that I was ready to leave, I decided that I had ridden long enough in nasty weather, for one day, so I used my cell phone to find the cheapest and closest motel. Once settled, I searched for the weather station on the television, and heard the commentator announce that the Midwest had been experiencing one of the coldest and wettest summers in history! The only thing that came to my mind was that it was just another part of "His" plan to strengthen my resolve. It was only too obvious that the weather would continue to be a threat throughout the rest of my tour, so I had to accept the challenge and continue on with a positive attitude. Since Mother Nature had a bad day and I had been caught up in her fury, it was sure nice to snuggle into a warm, dry, bed on that night!

I rode 104 miles on this day.

Sunday, June 28th, 2015   Day 18

I woke up feeling exhausted from a very noisy balcony party that went on all night at my choice of motel. It was too cold to start out early, so I passed the time cleaning my bike while I waited for the temperature to rise. By the time that I gassed up the bike's tank, it was still a bit cool, but comfortable enough with a couple of layers of clothes and the warmth of the sun, for me to continue onto my next destination.

When I got to Toledo, Ohio, my back was hurting more than usual from the cold, so I took a lunch break at a fast food restaurant. While in line to place my order, I shared my story with a curious woman standing behind me. While attempting to pay for my meal, another woman in the line told the cashier to put my lunch on her tab. It was a surprise, though a much appreciated one! My meal was satisfying and the rest felt good while warming up my bones! When leaving, with helmet in hand, I caught the interest of an older couple coming through the door. They inquired about my journey, so I shared some of my experiences with them. They had just come from church, so they were in their Sunday best. I commented on a beautiful pearl brooch that the woman was wearing. She immediately took it off and said: "Here, it's yours"! Being a Christian myself, I knew that her gracious generosity came straight from the heart and I accepted her gift with thanks. Sometimes we need to be reminded that the world is full of beautiful and selfless people. Keeping our hearts open will allow us to experience such goodness, even from complete strangers!

After riding several miles on 80/90 to Cleveland, I was becoming extremely hungry and knew that it was time to stop for dinner. I felt the need for some good, substantial nourishment, and was in hopes of a hot meal. I found that the toll road "Travel Centers" only offered very expensive, packaged, fast foods, so I decided to settle for some fresh fruit. I had been without it for several days, though when I realized that a cup of grapes would cost me $5, I could not justify purchasing them, while traveling on such a limited budget. That cash could buy me a tank of gas that would carry me 100 more miles! I was sifting through my groceries for something to put together for dinner in the parking lot when a couple showed an interest in the bumper sticker on my windshield. We began a conversation and I spoke with them about my frustration with the services offered at the food court. They immediately opened up the back of their vehicle and pulled out several trays of fruit, vegetables and sandwiches. They had just come from their daughter's catered wedding reception and were taking home leftovers, some of which they offered to me. I couldn't help but be amazed how my needs continued to be met by roadside "angels"! The meager meal that I had previously planned turned into a smorgasbord of delicious delights! I could not thank these strangers enough for their generosity.

I motored into a cold night, feeling ill from more vertigo symptoms and felt that a motel would, once again, be a necessity. As I rode, I calculated my finances with the hope that, soon, the weather would become more conducive to my budget. But for that one night I looked forward to the comfort of a hot meal and a warm room. A friend called later, and finding out about my plight, offered to pay for both! "Angels" were even coming to me through the cell phone towers!

I rode 248 miles on this day.

Monday, June 29th, 2015   Day 19

I was more than happy to rise early with plans to depart a very filthy and unpleasant motel in Akron, Ohio. The morning temperature was acceptable, though there was a threat of rain, so I was anxious to get some miles behind me. I pulled onto the interstate and was traveling at 70 mph when, after just 5 miles down the road, my bike lost all power and the engine died! I carefully coasted across two lanes of traffic before coming to a complete stop along the shoulder of the road. It was then that I remembered my experience in Traverse City, Michigan, when my neutral light had been flashing intermittently and the bike would not start. Instantly I knew that it must be connected to the problem at hand. I would have to deal with my breakdown by setting into motion whatever it would take to get me and my bike safely back on the road. I decided to first try and fix it on my own, so I got out my tools and set to work while being blasted by the wind of passing cars, trucks and tractor trailers. I quickly diagnosed that the problem was with my battery connection, but realized that I would not have the parts that I needed to do the repair. I called for roadside assistance and gave them my location. They said that it would be at least an hour before they could get someone out to me. Just as it began to rain, I looked up and saw a truck with flashing lights pulling up behind me. It was an insurance based roadside service operated by a young man who had a mechanical background. He took a look at my bike and agreed that it would have to be repaired at a motorcycle shop where they could supply the proper parts and tools that were needed. He then recommended that I take refuge in his truck while waiting, and I took him up on his offer. We passed the time sharing stories about our lives. He spoke of his 10 year old daughter, who suffered from Cerebral Palsy, and he told me what a source of joy and strength she was to him. He also revealed to me her love for dance, which tugged at my heart. The tow truck took over three hours to arrive, so I was thankful to this polite young man for keeping me safe, warm and dry. He was a safety road "angel" for sure!

The driver of the tow truck loaded up me and my bike and said that he would deliver us to the closest motorcycle shop in the area. It was quite a ways down the road, but once we got there and the bike was unloaded, the service manager put a mechanic on it immediately. He found that the positive wire to the battery was broken and that it had to be rewired. I waited around the shop, anxiously, visiting with the manager as the mechanic worked on the repair. After about two hours they test drove my bike, charged me a minimal fee for the work, and I was back on the pavement heading south.

I rode in a driving rain for 90 miles and was so cold that my hands and feet felt numb. After too many hours of miserable riding, I chose to stop, once again, at a motel. It was 10:30 pm by the time that I had my motorcycle gear unpacked and I was curled up in bed. Finally, I had come to the end of a very long and difficult day!

I rode 281 miles on this day.

Tuesday, June 30th, 2015   Day 20

I left the Beckley, Ohio, motel with the best intentions to have my tent set up at a campground long before dark. The motels had been less than satisfactory and I needed some human interaction that only camping could bring.

West Virginia offered interesting views and wild terrain. The dark tunnels were an unexpected surprise and actually a bit scary when riding through on a motorcycle. I felt as though I had lost all sense of space and direction, leaving me feeling totally out of control. And then to top it off, with my equilibrium problem, they were quite a challenge and extremely unsettling to say the least!

Probably the most frightening motorcycling experience that has ever happened to me was while riding through Virginia. I was traveling at 70 miles an hour in the center of a busy three lane interstate, when I began to feel a strange sensation in my head, not unlike what I had been dealing with throughout the whole trip, but this time it was coming on faster and was much more intense. Usually I had a warning when the vertigo spins were coming on, but this was different. All of a sudden it felt as if the road was coming up at me and as though I was swaying back and forth. I knew that I had to get to the shoulder as quickly as possible, but there was a semi-tractor trailer to my right, and cars approaching on my left. I slowed down to get behind the truck and moved over, braking as quickly and safely as possible to bring my bike to a stop on the side of the road. Just as I got the kickstand down, I slumped off of the bike and onto the pavement. Shaking and disoriented, I knew that there had to be divine intervention for me to have survived this terrifying and almost tragic experience. Just more proof that my "angels" had taken to the road with me!

After resting and getting past the adrenaline shakes, I knew that I had no choice but to pick myself up and get back in the saddle. With a long ride home ahead of me, I had to have faith that I would make it there safely. Even though my partner had told me, before I left on my journey, that he would come and get me at any time that I could not go on, it was clear to me that I had to persevere and accomplish the goal on my own.

After riding for a while, my legs began to feel tired, so I rested my feet on the highway pegs of my engine guards. (These are rounded metal bars that wrap around the front of the bike to protect legs and engine parts if the bike should go down. Years ago we called them "crash bars", though this description is no longer politically correct! Now they have a dual purpose, for they also provide a place to reposition tired legs on a long trip.) Within minutes the bars began to shake and rattle so I pulled off onto the side of the highway. Upon inspection, I found that the metal tubing had cracked in half at the weld where they were attached to the bike! This happened five years previously with the same brand of product and my local motorcycle dealer had exercised the warranty and installed new bars. There I was, once again, in the same situation, though a replacement would not be possible until I reached home. I knew that they would have to be removed by the original dealer or the warranty could not be guaranteed. I was destined to ride the remaining miles with broken guards, which not only compromised my initial comfort, but also my safety!

After passing through several more storms, I stopped at a gas station to rest and regroup. I was happy to be able to purchase some fresh fruit that had seemed to evade me along the way. I then washed it all down with a carrot and orange energy juice drink. Such simple sustenance could never have tasted so good! I visited with another veteran of  the road and she graciously snapped a photo to add to my collection of memories along my tour.

Soon there were clear, blue skies ahead and I felt that it was safe to remove all of my rain gear. This was always challenging when in a parking lot, since I had to take off my boots in order to remove my pants. My ballet training came into play when having to balance on one leg at a time! I was back on the highway for only 10 minutes and was hit again by another fast moving storm. Common sense told me to pull into a restaurant to avoid the oncoming tumultuous weather. There I enjoyed a fulfilling meal and some interesting conversation with a very cheerful waitress. It is amazing how much you can appreciate the friendliness of a stranger when so far away from familiarity and creature comforts!

As I left the restaurant I reached in my rain pants pocket for my motorcycle key and it was not there! I checked the bike ignition in hopes that I had just forgotten to remove it. Still no key. I began to panic and then remembered that, fortunately, I had thought ahead to bring another key along in case of just such a situation. I checked my pants once more and it was then that I realized that my brand new rain pants had a hole in the pocket and the key had fallen through it and into the inside lining of the pants! I had to cut along the seam with my pocket knife in order to retrieve the key. I was exuberant with relief!

At least the mystery was solved, but it could have been quite a different outcome. I had spent more than three months planning out my trip and it was worth all of the times that I woke up in the middle of the night with ideas of how to make it a total success without any mishaps. One important item that I had purchased was a "bra wallet" that hung by a Velcro strap at the center of my sports bra. In it I had placed my extra bike key, emergency phone numbers, a second credit card and cash. So if I lost my keys, phone or wallet, I would be totally covered. If not for recovering my key, this would have been the moment that made all of my planning worthwhile!

The most extreme torrential downpour, that I had ever experienced, during my 45 years of motorcycle riding, came next. After several miles of driving in heavy rain, I suddenly could not see anything in the front, back or side of the bike. I also knew that no one could see me, either! Finally, I got a slight glimpse of something green to my right and thought that it might be an exit sign, so I slowly transitioned and followed the pavement as best that I could. After getting off of the ramp, I prayed that I might find some kind of building or gas station where I could pull over, but to no avail. There wasn't even enough visibility to determine if the road had a substantial shoulder or if it just went down into a ditch, so I had to carry on into the abyss as I thought of an old, Russian proverb: "Pray to God, but continue rowing to shore!"

It seemed as if I rode on forever, up and down hills and around curves, navigating with very little or no clear vision when I spotted a faint light ahead of me. It was a small, one pump, gas station and country store. As I turned in, I almost rear-ended another motorcyclist. I then realized that he had been in front of me since getting off of the interstate. I could not even see his taillights through the pouring rain! We visited and shared our harrowing experience with hopes of never knowing one like it again. A young man came out of the station obviously sporting a very large firearm on his hip. The three of us had a discussion about weapon safety and gun laws. It was an interesting conversation to have with strangers, and I think that they were very surprised at my viewpoints and my willingness to be licensed and armed.

The other biker and I were both heading in the same direction that evening, so we decided to travel the next 50 miles together. After riding about 30 miles in a drizzling rain, I was so cold and wet that it became totally unbearable to continue on. At that point I waved him off, and exited the interstate. After stopping at a grocery store, I checked the radar on my cell phone and reluctantly decided that the approaching inclement weather would warrant another motel for the night. Once settling into my room, I noticed that my pony tail holder and braid had come out during the storm and my hair was in a tangled matted mess! With a length of 3 1/2 feet, it was no easy task to unravel. It kept me busy for hours before going to bed for a good night's sleep, after a long and eventful day.

I rode 265 miles on this day.

Wednesday, July 1st, 2015   Day 21

Asheville, North Carolina would be the next stop on my itinerary. It is touted as a mecca of artists that oozed with creative energy. As an artist myself, I had always felt drawn to visit there. Several times over the years I had researched information on its location and all that it had to offer, so I felt extremely disappointed as the weather disintegrated and I intentionally blew past the exit on the interstate to beat it as fast as I could to Franklin, North Carolina. Upon arrival, I would meet up with a friend that I met on a previous trip to the area. She had reserved me a site at a local campground that she highly recommended. I was excited to find out what new adventures might be waiting for me there.

It was a cool, and brisk morning with an aroma of wood smoke in the air as I wound around each curve and up over the steep hills. The exhilarating and refreshing ride felt more like fall than summer, at the foot of the majestic Smoky Mountains.

I found my friend at her office where we shared the latest news about our lives and looked forward to our visit during my stay. She then escorted me up to the campground where I was introduced to the owner and the site manager. I was warmly welcomed as they rolled out the red carpet treatment! A tarp was laid down for my tent and my bike was provided with its own undercover parking space. As I set up camp, I

felt incredibly impressed with the beauty and tranquility of the grounds and the wonderful hospitality that I was graced with. My friend made a generous donation toward my camping fees, which I did not find out about until my departure a week later. This gift was greatly appreciated and a testimony to her giving nature. Her "angel" qualities were definitely apparent!

While arranging my gear, I met up with a very "comical" gentleman and his beautiful wife. They would become a very large part of my most cherished memories at this amazingly, friendly, campground. This sweet, kind man took me on as his own personal project for worry. He was extremely concerned about me camping out in a tent with coyotes prowling around, let alone the inclement weather! I reassured him that I would be perfectly fine and that I was looking forward to the adventure. He kept a close watch on me, nonetheless.

I set up my tent and then rode to a health food store that I had seen on my way into town. I found a knowledgeable clerk there who shared some information on natural cures for vertigo. I had experienced it two other times throughout the years, but I knew that I was dealing with more than my past condition, so I did not have much faith with anything over the counter. After stuffing my saddlebag luggage full with groceries, I did some sightseeing and then returned to my campsite to unpack, when the rains came again!

I rode 99 miles on this day.

Thursday, July 2nd, 2015   Day 22

Even though I awoke to a slight, misty rain, I decided to go for a hike and do some exploring. From beneath my umbrella, I viewed quaint primitive cabins tucked under ancient trees. On one property there was a gem mine set up for the owner's private and personal use. There were ducks swimming in the pond, roosters crowing from the barn and crab apple trees in full bloom along a babbling brook. As I meandered, I felt as if I was in a dream world. Though as soon as I was on my way back to the camp, reality set in as I found myself swaying with dizziness. I could only remind myself that "this too shall pass".

At the campground I was approached by other campers who were worried about my welfare due to a storm that had passed through in the middle of the night. I had slept soundly through the thunder and lightning without any fear, though I was endeared by their concern. Thus, I knew that I was in good hands for the rest of my stay there.

The community center was surrounded by three walls with a built-in fire pit that was vented through the roof. In  the early morning, coffee drinkers gathered there to share in some friendly conversation. My comical, new friend seemed to be the focus with his many humorous quips.

Having been a veteran of the Girl Scouts, I immediately took it upon myself to start the first fire of the day. Impressed with my talent for fire building, my buddy decided that I should have the honor of starting it each morning while I was camped there. I was happy to oblige!

I spent the early part of that day cleaning the Virginia coal dust off of my motorcycle. It was in every nook and cranny! Although my bike was fourteen years old, and in mint condition before the departure of my tour, evident scars of accomplishment had begun to show up!

At lunchtime, I was back at my tent for a meal of grilled tofu and canned peas that I cooked over my camp stove. You can be very appreciative of such things when you become accustomed to the bare necessities. A few of my new friends stopped to chat and comment on my outdoor talents. After their visit, I enjoyed a nice rest and felt totally at peace in my world.

I could not get any cell phone service near my tent and I needed to check in with my partner, so I went up to the campground office to find out what the protocol was for communication with the outside world. The manager told me to "walk up the hill" and "stand on the big rock on the corner". I know that I can be gullible at times, but this could top it all! He swore that it was true, so I took off in the rain for the "rock phone service" on the hill! Amazingly it did work. I was able to get out a short call, though I had to turn my head in just the right direction and talk fast, for the service was continuously dropped. After several attempts, my partner and I were able to piece together somewhat of a conversation before we became totally frustrated and said our goodbyes.

On the way back to the campground, I saw a couple of people crawling in and out of a brushy thicket. Upon inquiring, they said that they were picking wild berries. I decided to put that on my "to do" list if it should ever quit raining!

I had a dinner of canned black beans with rice, and then took a hike along a wet and mountainous path. While I wandered, I reminisced of my experiences thus far, and of the unending strength and perseverance that I had gained along the way. As I fell off to sleep that night, I felt safe, secure and fulfilled.

No miles were ridden on this day.

Friday, July 3rd, 2015   Day 23

After a cold, damp, night in my tent, I was building the morning fire when my friend arrived with his coffee in hand. He was happy to see that I was up for my task on such a chilly morning. Building and lighting a fire was the only possible way for me to get warm, so I was happy to accommodate him!

Several folks began to gather and, once again, the main flow of conversation was about how bad they felt for my situation. It had been raining and consistently cold since I had arrived, and the fact that I was the only one tent camping made them all sympathetic. I was just happy to be sitting still for a few days without any pressure to get back on the road!

While doing some maintenance on my bike, I noticed a middle-aged couple loading up their motorcycle with gear. They seemed to be a bit antagonistic with each other and it made me feel uncomfortable, since I am not one to argue or share my grievances in a public place. The guy was being verbally abusive with his companion and I could sense her humiliation as she tried to avoid eye contact with me. Later in the day she approached me and asked if we could talk. She wanted to know where I pulled my strength from to be so independent and brave. She felt that she could never go it alone, without a man, though wished that she could somehow find a way. She knew that her relationship was not healthy, and that she needed to get out of it, but was unsure of how to leave safely. We talked, while her companion hovered nearby, obviously wary of what looked like a newfound friendship. As she excused herself to return with him to their camper, I could only hope that she would find the courage to get some professional help in order to someday escape his control.

Later in the afternoon, there was a short break in the weather, so I thought that I should take the opportunity to venture outdoors. I had seen some panning supplies in the shed behind the community center, so gathering them up, I set out for the river to give it a try. The water was cold and knee deep, though I had a great time sifting sandy silt through my pan while searching for the gems that the area

was often known to give up. Though I did not find any treasure that would change my financial status, I did procure several rocks that could make some beautiful jewelry! Just when I thought that I was finished hunting, a guy began working next to me with a different kind of pan than I was using. When I asked him about it he said that it was exclusively for panning gold and proceeded to give me a lesson in finding some. It is a very long, drawn out, and tedious process that takes a lot of patience. I am not sure how they did it, day in and day out, during the "Gold Rush"!

It had been a fun, interesting, eventful, and yet another wet day in North Carolina!

No miles were ridden on this day.

Saturday, July 4th, 2015   Day 24

After the morning fire was blazing hot, I curled up on a bench next to it and began writing in my journal. So much had happened since leaving my home on June 11th. My journey had taken me across many miles and smiles and it was all that I could ever have imagined or hoped for. While in deep thought, I anticipated what kind of adventure might lie ahead with the terrain that I was yet to cover. Before leaving on my tour, a friend of mine asked how I could take off alone and travel so far from home. I told her that I would get up each day and think of it as if I was just on another motorcycle ride, only starting and ending in a different place!

Another morning walk, in the rain, took me up a rocky road lined with fences that surrounded cows and donkeys.

The animals seemed at peace in their serene setting and were very interested in me, this strange, human creature walking along on two legs. I took my time, as I inhaled every minute detail, for the scenery was spectacular and deserved my undivided attention!

While visiting with others back at the camp, I was invited to the annual 4th of July pot luck dinner, followed by fireworks. We gathered together at the clubhouse, where we shared in prayer and feasted on homemade goodies. It was a lively and fun filled gathering with wonderful people, and I enjoyed it tremendously!

As darkness set in, chairs were lined up along the road just below a bridge, where the fireworks were lit and an amazing explosion lit up the sky. For more than an hour we oohed and awed over the spectacular show. It was the most amazing display that I had ever seen up close. These folks knew how to celebrate the holiday!

No miles were ridden on this day.

Sunday, July 5th, 2015   Day 25

Though my every intention was to stay until the end of the week in North Carolina, I awoke on that morning with an urge to move on. Sometimes you just know in your gut that it is time to leave. The dampness and cold were getting to me and I hoped that it would be warmer and drier as soon as I headed south. My riding jeans had been hung near the fire pit in the clubhouse for 5 days and they were showing no signs of drying out with the sun hiding behind the ever existing clouds!

I pulled on my damp jeans over dry insulated tights, and had just begun packing up my bike, when one of the other campers approached. She had breakfast ready for me and insisted that I return to her motorhome where I feasted on a tasty meal fit for a queen! As I walked back to my bike, I contemplated on how such kind hospitality would make my departure even more bittersweet. I knew that I would never forget how well I had been cared for, while a guest at such a special place, and hoped that someday I might be able to return for a stay in the future.

After goodbyes and well wishes from my new found friends, I headed out toward the Highlands, a unique and upscale community that was at a much higher altitude than from where I had come. It was definitely uphill all the way with many twists and turns, creating another challenge for me from the weight of the luggage pack that I carried on the back of my bike. I continued on up to the waterfalls that I was told not to miss before leaving

the state. I was very uncomfortable when I had to navigate a vertical incline coming into the parking lot to view some of the falls, and once parked, I decided to reconsider. After a much closer look, I quickly came to the realization that my vertigo was not going to allow me the privilege of safely hiking the steep trails to take the complete tour. Though disappointed, what I was able to view from my standpoint was an amazing show of Mother Nature at her best!

The next 100 miles of scenic back roads, that should have only taken me two hours by interstate highway, took four hours because of their poor condition and disrepair! I considered changing my route as I dodged "black road snakes" (slippery tar patches), potholes, and ruts in the road, but I had dinner plans with a friend in Abbeville, South Carolina, so I decided to stay on my mapped out course. I reached my planned destination a bit tired, but I was thrilled to enjoy a hot meal with good company. Though we had not been in contact with each other for  over 21 years, that visit would prove to be a healing meeting of the minds that was destined to bring some much needed and long awaited closure to us both.

I rode 110 miles on this day.

Monday, July 6th, 2015   Day 26

After riding several miles, I saw a gas station with a picnic table along the side of the road. I was hungry and in search of some fresh fruit, and although I knew that it would be ridiculously priced, I was hopeful that I might find some there. After purchasing a banana and an apple for more than I would like to admit, I perched myself up on the table and ate my breakfast while soaking in some warm morning rays.

My eyes had been extremely itchy and irritated while riding, so I was curious as to what might be in the air. An older gentleman asked if he could share a bench with me, so I moved over and we began to visit. He went on to tell me about how all of his adult life he had worked in the granite mines as a "cutter", carving out tombstones from raw granite. He noticed that I was rubbing my eyes and told me that I was suffering from the granite dust that floated in the air from the mine that I had just passed a mile down the road. I was happy to have found out the cause, and also anxious to leave Sweet City, Georgia, as soon as possible, to relieve my discomfort. Just then another motorcycle enthusiast rode up on his bike and I found myself engaged in more conversation. He was enthralled with my story of where I had come from and how far I still had to travel. He knew the dangers and discomforts of a long motorcycle road trip and expressed his admiration for my show of courage and determination.

At lunch time I pulled off after spotting a grocery store that advertised a health oriented deli and snack bar. I was really looking forward to having my favorite herbal tea drink, along with a filling meal, and I was pretty sure that I might find it there. I began to feel the hunger pangs slowly fade while I enjoyed the last of my nutritious dinner. Just as

I was about to finish up and move on, I was befriended by two elderly gentlemen who seemed very interested in my pursuit. While parked in the grocery store lot, they had seen  the sticker on the backrest of my motorcycle and hoped that they might meet up with the owner of the bike, but they did not ever expect to find out that it belonged to a woman rider. They asked if I would join them and share the details of my cause. We talked about many of life's trials and tribulations, but mostly about one of the gentleman's issues with his children, who happened to be adults over 40 years old. He spoke of how he could not live his life as he pleased because of their controlling behavior and his inability to stand up to them. As I was leaving, he made a pact with himself that he would buy his dream motorcycle and hit the road before it was too late for him. I would later receive word from his friend that he had become ill within days of his pledge and would not be going through with his plan. How sad that he had waited too long to live his life as he chose.

More storms were approaching and I needed to make a decision about lodging for the night. Just then a lightning bolt struck much too close for comfort, making it easy to cut my ride short and pull off to the first motel in sight! I found it to be affordable, so I settled in with anticipation of the next day and what it might bring.

I rode 187 miles on this day.

Tuesday, July 7th, 2015   Day 27

I was on the road early, for I was extremely anxious to reach the Florida and Georgia border, though I was not prepared for the feelings that rushed through me. As I approached the line between the two states, I felt raw, bittersweet emotion at the realization that I was almost home. It had been a difficult journey, though the wonders never ceased as I covered the miles and reveled in the experiences.

The Florida welcome center was a good transition point, where I spent some time passing out the last of my bumper stickers and cards while speaking with many people about my quest and adventure. They all showed great interest and made my time and effort all the more promising. Before leaving, I took a break and rested at a picnic table under a shade tree. I phoned a friend who had been a big supporter of my cross-country motorcycle tour, from Indiana to California and back, when I was only 23 years old. As we reminisced of past times and of the years that had flown by, he reminded me of my courage, those many years ago, and of how I had made that long journey on a much smaller motorcycle, completing the trip in just two weeks, traveling 500 miles per day! It thrilled him that my youthful and courageous free spirit was still intact. Recently he had given up his motorcycle for fear of aging and lack of reaction time, though he felt fortunate that he could travel vicariously through me.

I left the rest stop with the drive to push on to my next destination. Storms were building to the south displaying a spectacular and dramatic sky. I felt that I had gone as far as I could safely, without rain gear, and pulled off under a bridge where I would have dry cover to change into my jacket, pants, boot covers and reflective vest. As soon as I parked, I realized that I had arrived at the last point of my adventure, and from then on I would be in all too familiar territory. The thrill of the unknown would be over. I was not ready to end my journey, though I knew that it would have to come to a close sooner or later. I had a feeling of great loss that I would not be there in that moment, ever again. My only conciliation, when I pulled back onto the highway, was the sense of fulfillment and pride that I felt from accomplishing my goal.

Later, I would receive an email from a very dear friend, to let me know that while also returning from a trip, she had passed by me as I was resting under the bridge. After having read about my quest, online, it was exciting for her to have spotted me along the highway, and she tried to phone in order that we might be able to meet up for dinner. Although trying frantically, she could not get the call to go through. After many attempts, she felt that she had gone too far to turn back, and though terribly disappointed that we had been unable to connect, she was thrilled to see that I had made it safely back into the state of Florida. Later, she realized that she had been dialing the wrong number! Just the coincidence of seeing me there, along the road, seemed to console her in the end. We both were able to enjoy a good laugh over her cellphone blunder!

My closest friends and family have long known my love for the naturalist lifestyle, so it would be of no surprise to them that I had decided to wind down from my tour back at the nudist resort. When there, my free spirit is alive and well in a place where I can relax, spend quiet time and be creative. So after hours of riding through more tumultuous weather, I found myself safe, sound, and naked at my favorite nudist resort in Lutz, Florida! As I set up my tent and prepared the campsite, I was welcomed back by all of my friends who had anxiously awaited my return. It was also a very pleasant surprise when the staff notified me that they were generously donating my camping fees for the week. It became clearly obvious to me that "angels" are not always clothed in long, white, cascading robes!

I rode 354 miles on this day.

Wednesday, July 8th, 2015   Day 28

I crawled out of my tent with oatmeal and hot tea on my mind, so I set up the cooker on the picnic table and began preparing breakfast. Many of my friends stopped by to hear about my adventures and congratulate me on my successful journey.

A morning hike was the next thing on my agenda, so I donned a hat and sneakers and took off for the trail around the lake. There are over 200 acres of nature trails that have been inhabited by hand carved sculptures which peek out from behind tree trunks and hang from their branches. It is always fun to find the newest additions to the woods. A resident artist is the source of these creations and his works bring pleasure to all who cross their paths.

By noon I was enjoying the pool, sauna and hot tub, in that order. I spent quite a while chatting with a visiting psychologist. We spoke of the "common sense of life" and I found it to be an enriching exchange of philosophy that left me with much to think about!

Upon returning to my campsite, I relaxed with a bottle of kombucha. When a friend of mine stopped by, I introduced him to the drink and he was immediately hooked! It is an organic, raw, fermented herbal tea and a living food that is chockfull of enzymes, probiotics and polyphenols that are extremely beneficial to good health!

In the afternoon, I pulled one of the complimentary kayaks down to the beach where I met another camper getting ready to go out onto the lake. We paddled across to the entrance of a channel that would take us through the cypress tree knees. It was an overhead jungle and a difficult passage, but well worth the challenge, as we paddled back out into an amazing sunset!

While traveling, I had been trying to maintain my ballet work outs and it was time to get back into my pointe shoes, so I headed up to the outdoor stage where I had danced many times in the past. It was on that evening that I did my "Ballet in the Buff" performance!

What a wonderfully freeing day it was, and as I began to prepare for bed, I realized just how difficult it would be to reenter the "real world" upon my return home.

No miles were ridden on this day.

Thursday, July 9th, 2015   Day 29

I had plans to hike that morning with a camper who was tented next to me. My balance had become increasingly more unstable, so I had a difficult time keeping up with him while trying to walk a straight line! Though I struggled some, I did complete the whole distance of the nature trails and felt good for it.

Along the trail is a wooden "angel" that is nailed to the trunk of a tree. It was about three years ago that I first spotted the angel. She looked a bit pitiful to me, for she had

been cut from wood that had aged and obviously been charred by fire. After some investigation, I found out that the main caretaker of the resort property had pulled her out of a cooling morning campfire, and the fact that she had survived made him feel the need to find her a home. One afternoon I took my box of paints out into the woods and brought her back to life. My mother had recently passed, so I painted her in the image of my mom. I also gave her a beautiful violet gown and silvery angelic wings. It always gives me great pleasure to see her each time that I hike the nature trails while camping there.

After walking with my friend, I returned to my campsite for lunch. Feeling totally at peace, I just sat at the picnic table and watched the world go by. There was no need to do anything but relax, so that was just exactly what I did!

I really looked forward to doing some bass fishing, since I had experienced some extremely good luck while fishing there in the past. My rod had been broken during the trip, so after a swim in the pool, I set off on my bike in search of a sporting goods shop. I was certainly thrilled when I found the perfect folding rod and reel set! Upon leaving the store, I saw that another storm was forming low on the horizon so I high tailed it back to the resort.

After the rains had passed, I started a camp fire in the barbeque pit, and along with a couple of friends, we roasted tofu hot dogs and marshmallows. Somehow a gathering of campers always seems to initiate some good conversation and belly laughs!

I wanted to do another ballet workout, but since it was already dark, I decided to do it in the community center instead of on the outdoor stage. Unexpectedly, I soon found that I had an audience. After I danced to a few songs, a gentleman, who had been working on a computer in the back of the room, began to clap. I went over to him to introduce myself when I realized that he could not speak or hear. Though we were unable to have a conversation, we managed to communicate on a much deeper level. He had enjoyed my performance and I had been rewarded with his joy! This gentleman was very confident in himself and managed to draw others into his world with his positive, friendly, and upbeat personality. "Angels" can appear to us when we speak silently, and listen with our open hearts!

When I was just 16 years old, and in my freshman year of high school, I had a history teacher that I truly adored. He understood me unlike any of my other instructors. One day I had to give a talk in front of the class, and when I had finished, he said: "Miss Sullivan (my maiden name) you sure do dance to the beat of a very different drummer!" I was devastated and wanted to crawl under my desk! No teenager wanted to be singled out as being different from the rest. To the contrary, every effort was made to, hopefully, fit in. At that time I did not realize how blessed I was to be a unique, free spirit in a world where I seldom would be accepted by society's standards. There are many who "dance to the beat of a different drummer", but it is the fortunate ones who accept their uniqueness as a gift and use it as a way to bless others!

The hot tub seemed like a perfect way to end the day, so I spent some time there relaxing and visiting with more of my friends. One of them was also camped nearby, so we walked back to the campsite together, where we sat at the picnic table discussing the affairs of the human race. When we had exhausted our attempts to find answers for saving the world, we retired to our respective tents. I read from "Walden" until fatigue set in and I fell into a sound sleep.

I rode 27 miles on this day.

Friday, July 10th, 2015   Day 30

I could hardly wait to go fishing with my new rod and reel, so I woke up early. I would have to give in to getting dressed on that morning, since fishing can be a dangerous sport with hooks, fins and teeth that could injure tender body parts! After having breakfast, I headed down to the beach. Several casts later, I had not even one nibble and was beginning to think that my previous luck with the bass had surely run out. A friend who saw that I wasn't having any success, came by to offer me a "special" rubber worm. He showed me how to hook it up "Texas style". This trick was taught to him by his father and he swore to its ability to catch fish. Next, I moved on to one of my favorite spots where there was a deep bass hole down by the boat ramp. After having literally no luck there, I decided to try the new

floating docks by the pool. It was then that I hooked into "the big one"! I fought it hard and long, but eventually it snapped my line in two. What a thrill I had trying to bring that one in! Earlier, I had noticed that one of my fishing friends was out in his boat, across the lake. He motored over to tell me that he had lit into a school of bass and invited me aboard to go after more. We had a great time as the bass were so thick that they just about jumped into the boat for our taking. My new rod and reel were well initiated on that morning!

The resort was sponsoring a Christian nudist group the whole week that I was there, with many group functions that related to their association. They were some of the nicest and most intuitive people that I had ever met, and I enjoyed finding out more information about them. One of the members was camped close to me, and he shared a lot of their insights on that afternoon.

Later, while perched on the picnic table with a book, I felt an itching sensation on my right thigh, just above the knee. My first thought was that I had been bitten by a bug. Upon examining the suspected bite, I felt a sense of panic as I identified it as another possible skin cancer lesion. There had not been any sign of it the day before and here it was, very red, raised and misshapen! More often than not, they are questionable with the need for a biopsy to determine if they are malignant or benign, but this time I already knew that I would be facing another surgery. It had come up too quick and looked too angry for it to be anything else. I had been dealing with skin cancer for the past seven years, with as many surgeries, and had become quite adept to being able to identify them. My dermatologist and I have had an ongoing joke that I am quicker at catching them than she is! Though a veteran of the disease, the thought of another diagnosis and surgery was very disturbing. You could never know when the next one might be life threatening! I would have to contact my dermatologist as soon as I arrived home.

I contemplated what more could possibly go wrong, at this point, with all that I had already gone through and what still lay ahead. I have always respected this quote by Plato: "Be kind, for everyone you meet is fighting a great battle!"

That evening I joined my friends up at the snack bar. The original restaurant had been demolished in preparation for new construction, so a temporary food stand had been brought in to cover the need. We sat down at picnic tables covered with red checkered cloths, while the chef made me a dinner of my favorite veggie burger salad. I could not think of a better way to end a wonderful day full of fun, fellowship and adventure!

No miles were ridden on this day.

Saturday, July 11th, 2015   Day 31

The resort was updating their advertisement and had announced that a group photo would be taken poolside. There was also a festival planned on the grounds, by the lake, that would include live music along with arts and crafts vendors, and I was looking quite forward to joining in the celebration.

At 2:00 in the afternoon, 258 nudists filled the pool for the photo shoot. With the photographer perched on a tall ladder, the infamous shot was taken and I was there to become a part of the resort's history. I was totally in my comfort zone having spent years doing artistic nude shoots and modeling for art studios!

Later in the day, I got back into the pool to do a workout. After my normal 30 minutes of water aerobics, I was resting along the side of the pool, when suddenly I began to feel nauseous and flushed, along with chest pain and a dull ache that ran from my left shoulder down to my fingertips. My mind instantly traveled back, to years earlier, when I had suffered a Myocardial Infarction (mild heart attack) with similar symptoms that had landed me in the hospital. I felt numb with fear and instantly thought of how this could be the end of my motorcycle tour! The disappointment would be unbearable after all that I had already endured to bring it to completion. Just as I began to turn to someone for help, the symptoms began to subside. I knew, logically, that I should have headed to the nearest hospital emergency room, but denial came into play and I put the experience on the back burner to address later. It had been too amazing of a trip to be ruined by such reality, allowing me to justify my decision not to take further action, until I returned home.

That night there was a band and dancing at the "Butt Hut". They had a black light, right out of the 70's, and jars of iridescent paint available for body painting. Everyone had a wonderfully good time being creative, but I was especially impressed with a couple who had painted each other as native Indians. They looked amazingly authentic in their tribal birthday suits!

I always look forward to meeting up with a friend of mine on dance nights at the resort. She is a strikingly beautiful woman from the islands. Her bronzed skin is always draped in a skimpy sarong and she wears a fresh, red Hibiscus flower in her hair. She is also the most incredible dancer that I have ever known. We always enjoy tearing up the dance floor together and that night was no different, except for the vertigo that endowed me with a few extra moves!

The hot tub never felt as good as it did after hours of kicking up my heels. Once relaxed, I walked back to my tent and tucked myself in. There was a group of people sitting at a nearby campfire, and just as I was falling off to sleep, they got really cranked up! I was exhausted, but knew that there would be no rest until their party came to a close. The noise curfew was at 11:00 pm, so by 11:30 I had become frustrated enough to put a call through to the resort's front office. The manager sent the security guard over to remind the group that it was time to quiet down. Minutes later, I heard them proclaim: "let's burn down the ballerina's tent with her inside!" They knew that it was me who had called in the complaint, since I was the only camper that had not joined them around the fire. Panic and fear arose in me. I had never seen these people at the resort before, and did not know what they were capable of doing. I then called security direct and when the officer came, he immediately dispersed them to their camp sites. He then watched over me for the rest of the night. The next morning I found out that they were only members of the festival crew, who were just passing through, and were not known regulars of the resort. Though, once again, I was being threatened by inebriated people whose "liquid courage" made them dangerous! With the fire extinguished, and the offenders passed out in their tents, I fell into a fitful and restless sleep.

No miles were ridden on this day.

Sunday, July 12th, 2015   Day 32

It was my day of departure and I awoke early to more storm clouds, so I hustled to knock down my tent and pack up my gear. I had made many new friends, and had also enjoyed the company of my old ones, so I felt sad about saying goodbye, even though I knew that I would return, again, sometime in the future.

Once on the road, with the final miles of my trip ahead of me, I flashed back to all of the wonderful experiences that had changed my life forever. I also thought about how, unexpectedly, I had received the added bonuses of personal strength and healing that would carry me through difficult times to come. During my journey, I had stood up with a firearm to protect myself from a violent stranger, I had navigated rough and treacherous terrain, I had been plunged into memories of great loss, I had found closure for the little girl who could not fight back, I had forgiven past hurts, I did not quit when the going got tough and I persevered against all odds. I found out how strong and resilient I could be and that I had not lost the ability to accomplish anything that I set my mind to do. My mother always said: "Never, ever, underestimate that girl!" Now I would look forward to my future filled with new meaning and reverence.

After living for a month with the bare necessities of just a small tent and two duffle bags, I realized the need and desire to further simplify my life upon my return home. I also made the decision to exclude all drugs from my treatment program that had only been a detriment to my health. Instead, I would pursue the natural route with a balanced diet, power juicing and weight bearing exercise. Hopefully, I would be rewarded with stronger bone density and a more positive diagnosis in the years to come.

As I reached my exit and left the interstate toward home, the only thing on my mind was the reunion with my partner. I had been away from him for a month while I was on tour, and missed him terribly. I could hardly wait to be in his comforting arms again. As soon as he  arrived at my door and we embraced, I knew that I would be looking forward to our motorcycling journeys, together, in the future.

I rode 88 miles on this last day.

Mileage at departure: 10,107
Mileage upon arrival: 14061

Total miles traveled: 3,954!

LESSONS THAT I LEARNED ALONG THE WAY

Suit up in rain gear before you see lit headlights coming at you.

It is not a good idea to sneeze with your face shield down!

Carry along a tub stopper. Motels have eliminated them.

Being armed with a weapon can come in handy!

Soak your tent with silicone spray, since you can't ever be too dry.

Bring along some kind of gadgets to lock your tent zippers.

You cannot have too many straps holding down your gear.

An I pod is a must if you prefer to not listen to yourself sing!

On the backroads, don't count on the next gas station being there.

Paper maps are more reliable than GPS.

Watch out for "black road snakes"!

Mother Nature can have more than one bad day!

Cell phone radar is not always a reliable source.

Never trust someone giving you directions when you are lost!

You can carry on a conversation with a machine when very lonely.

Most people are generally good.

You are much stronger than you believe to be true.

Those closest to your heart will be there for you when in need.

Every day brings a blessing.

Strangers can be "angels" in disguise!

EPILOGUE

Osteoporosis is a cruel and disabling disease affecting many people who feel hopeless with their diagnosis. The intention of my tour was to educate the public, renew the faith of those affected, and to give me the will to fight for my life. Hopefully my story has inspired all of you, who have enjoyed the journey, for now I truly believe that I have accomplished what I set out to do!

Since returning, I have made numerous changes in my choices of foods and their preparation. Though I have been conscious of my nutrition for years, and have made every effort to eat properly, I knew that I could come up with some definite improvements. I admit that I had become somewhat remiss at times, in order to keep up with the demands of every day obligations, though now I make my health requirements the main priority. It takes a lot more time and energy, and I must be diligent, but it will be well worth it if my condition improves against all odds. One very important decision that I have made is to totally eliminate all synthetic supplements and replace them with whole natural products. I am now baking egg shells and grinding them into a fine powder, which is a great form of calcium that I am able to sprinkle on all of my meals. The food does have a gritty texture, but I have become accustomed to it. Also nutritious are the flax, chia, sunflower and pumpkin seeds, along with the walnuts and almonds that I blend together to make my creamy and delicious "nut milk", which I enjoy every morning. One day I was reading about the importance of eating sardines for healthy bone development. Just the thought of them triggered my gag reflex, though I decided that I would try to tolerate them, nonetheless. That same day while riding my bicycle, I passed a picnic table with a brand new unopened can of sardines sitting in plain view, with no one around to claim them. Now if that isn't divine intervention, I don't know what is! Growing my own live Scobie mushrooms (healthy bacterial culture) and brewing kombucha tea with them at home, has saved me the expense of the store bought products, allowing me to partake of it every day. I no longer purchase pre-prepared or refined foods, and I avoid using a microwave. I buy my beans, legumes, rice, oats, quinoa and millet in bulk and then cook them on the stove top. I indulge in "baked oatmeal bars" daily, which are my own recipe that include numerous healthy and nutritional ingredients that replace the popular energy bars that have a high sugar content. With all of these changes and a predominantly plant based diet full of fruits, vegetables, nuts, seeds, legumes, sprouts, leafy greens, grains, and beans, I believe that I am doing all that I can to hopefully overcome the Osteoporosis that is threatening to shorten my life.

Following an appointment with my dermatologist, and a biopsy, I was diagnosed with a Squamous Cell Carcinoma on my leg. Surgery was scheduled immediately, and afterwards I was shocked and dismayed as I was told to elevate my leg, and to stay totally off of it for two weeks! It seems that legs are much harder to heal, and the location of the lesion, being over my thigh muscle, extended the normal time frame for healing. It actually took months before the pain ceased and I was able to dance again. Too often, skin cancer is just considered an aggravating side effect of living in "paradise". Even though it seems normal to observe a large part of Florida's population sporting their "biopsy band aids", it still must be taken seriously, acknowledging the danger, and staying diligent with yearly skin checkups.

The vertigo and instability became increasingly worse upon my return, so I was referred to a neurologist by my primary care physician. He diagnosed a brain injury which was caused by the blow to my head one week before the departure of my trip. I was prescribed an anti-seizure drug that would help to stabilize my gait and terminate my dizzy spells. Unfortunately, I would have to take the drug for the rest of my life, but I was relieved to know that there was a solution to such a debilitating condition.

Two weeks after my tour, I had a total collapse with heart symptoms that placed me in the hospital for three days. Upon describing the pool incident to my cardiologist, he agreed with me that I, most likely, had another Myocardial Infarction on that day, with the most recent incident being complicated by some rapid heartbeat arrhythmias. I was prescribed preventative medication for both conditions and have had no further issues.

An illness that I did not speak of during my trip, though of which was weighing very heavily on me, was a diagnosis that came on the same day that I had been diagnosed with the advanced case of Osteoporosis. My yearly mammogram had come back with an abnormality that needed to be addressed. Every woman lives her whole life with the fear of such a phone call and I had unfortunately received mine. An MRI directed, Core Needle Biopsy diagnosed me with Pseudo Angiomatous Stromal Hyperplasia, an uncommon type of breast disease. Though the tumors from this disease are generally benign, they can mimic cancer, hide cancer, or give it a cozy place to thrive overtime. So basically I have felt that I am living with a time bomb in my breast! I have had a Lumpectomy to remove the original tumor and another miserable biopsy that resulted in the diagnosis of an additional tumor. I am only including this information about my health because of my most recent visit to the women's breast health center where I had to go for further testing. Even though my disease does not hold the same clout as breast cancer (insurance companies do not recognize it or have protocol to provide for a cure, which would mean a bilateral mastectomy), I still suffer with some of the same treatments and constantly live with the ongoing fear of future developments. While waiting for my turn outside of the mammogram exam room, I felt the emotional pain of all of the women waiting with me. On each and every one of their faces was written a sense of apprehension. It seemed that even looking up and making eye contact with another patient might mean having to acknowledge that their worst fear could come true. It doesn't matter if it is your first experience with breast disease, or your last, you will always relive the terror of the first day that you were diagnosed, when walking through those clinic doors. As I write this, I am awaiting the call from my surgeon that may possibly mean another disfiguring surgery for me. I hope that through this book I might reach out and inspire the tribe of women warriors that I so identify with. I may not have earned the "pink ribbon", since thankfully, I am not yet a "breast cancer patient", but I do feel as though I belong with the "survivors", since with each tumor that has to be surgically removed, I pray that I will have dodged another bullet!

With all of the negative forces against me, I believe that it was my faith in God and my strong will that kept me going, and allowed me to continue my tour without a major mishap. We never know why we are chosen to endure such calamities, but through this difficult process I have come to believe that illness can become a gift that sharpens your mind, clarifies your thoughts, and enriches your life, thus allowing you to inspire others. Without my health struggles and the level of despair that I have found myself in, I could not have written this book.

Most recently, I was having this same discussion with one of my dear friends at a local health food store, when a heavenly light went off in my head. Jesus was chosen to walk the earth, sharing his faith and love of God without the promise of longevity. He suffered and died a young man, though not without leaving a legacy of knowledge and inspiration. I would like to believe that we, also, in some ways, have been chosen for a likely purpose. I decided years ago, before all of this anguish had been bestowed upon me, that I would live each day as a "Good Will Ambassador", and I have done just that. Never will I let a day go by without making an effort to demonstrate unconditional love by the simple action of hugging a total stranger, paying someone a compliment or sharing my life experiences. You never know how you may have touched a lonely heart, brought up a level of confidence, or planted a much needed seed. If everyone exercised these qualities daily, imagine what a wonderful world this would be!

As for how I relate to life and death, I can only believe that a shorter time on earth, means a longer stay in heaven!

THE END

Angels Are Watching Over You

God has sent His angels
To gather here on earth
And surround us with their presence
From the moment of our birth

I believe they intercede
And often times appear
To protect us in our time of need
Guardian angels always near

So never fear what lies ahead
As you travel each day through
For there are angels by your side
Watching over you.

ACKNOWLEDGEMENTS

I want to thank everyone from the bottom of my heart, especially Christine, who helped to make my Face The Fear Tour possible. Without all of you, it could not have come to fruition. Your belief in my quest, and your generous donations helped to carry me through the trials and tribulations of such a momentous challenge. Any of my friends and angels that have been described in this book have remained anonymous to protect their privacy, but you know who you are!

Many, many thanks to Melodie, my friend, neighbor, art student and studio assistant for all of her love, advice, support and patience during the many hours of editing that it took in order to help me put my journey into print.

Thanks to my long, time friend, Jeane, who was always there for me with her spiritual knowledge and insight, listening to my endless ramblings, as I sorted out my inner thoughts.

I also want to thank Jason for bringing forth his technical skills to help me prepare this book for publishing. I could not have done it without his guidance.

Most of all, I am so thankful for my partner, Jim, who is my best friend and confidant. He was there for me every step of the way, through the laughter and the tears. Even as the miles between us grew longer I knew that he was just a phone call away. Never does a day go by that he doesn't say: "I'm right here, if you need me".

HEAVENLY THANKS BE TO GOD

For the many gifts and talents that He has bestowed upon me. His messages were loud, and His direction was clear. All that I had to do was to listen quietly, and follow the path that He laid out for me.

ABOUT THE AUTHOR

Nancy Taylor is an artist, model, author and ballerina residing in Venice, Florida. She leads an active lifestyle motorcycling, boating, fishing, bicycling, kayaking, swimming, hiking and dancing. Every day is an adventure with no time to waste. When not on the go, she works in her home at "Studio Sea Gallery", where she teaches art classes and sells her fine art and gifts.

For book orders, speaking engagements, or inquiries please contact the author at: ntaylorart@yahoo.com

Back cover photo by: Joseph De Sciose